Advance Praise

"Agility is the most decisive factor in successfully navigating the Fourth Industrial Revolution and fulfilling its promise to humankind. In this important and compelling book, Tilman and Jacoby provide a comprehensive theory of agility and a practical guide to developing and leading agile organizations."

—Klaus Schwab, Founder & Executive Chairman, World Economic Forum

"A significant contribution to leadership thinking at a time of increasing complexity, intense scrutiny, and rapid change. Recognizing agility as an essential driver of success in business, industry, and the military is vital. Understanding how to foster and consistently deliver it is even more critical. This must-read book helps us achieve both."

—Martin Dempsey, 18th Chairman of the Joint Chiefs of Staff

"This is a thoughtfully written book and one that will make the reader think. It makes you ask fundamental questions about the business you are in. Above all, it both broadens and sharpens the definition of what it means to be agile. Drawing on a rich set of historical and current examples from the private and public sectors as well as the military, the authors lucidly illustrate a framework that will be useful to leaders of all types of organizations in a time of accelerated change and adaptation."

—Lakshmi Shyam-Sunder, Chief Risk Officer, World Bank Group

"All leaders are facing an era of rapid change. That's true across politics, the military, all areas of business and every geography. We are all asking ourselves how we can lead successfully as we deal with fast-moving events, ambiguity, uncertainty and volatility. Tilman and General Jacoby skillfully present clear and reasoned strategies for anyone interested in learning and applying organizational agility to get ahead and prosper in this age of disruption."

—Doug Peterson, President and CEO, S&P Global

"In business, government, and warfare, agility is critical to survival, competitiveness, and enduring success. This original and practical book is a must-read for the leaders of organizations and teams who want to really understand what it means and what it takes to be agile."

—John Abizaid, US Ambassador to Saudi Arabia

"The future belongs to agile organizations. With a rare clarity of thought and a wealth of experience, Tilman and Jacoby have given us an invaluable roadmap to how such organizations can be built and nurtured for the long-term."

—George Mitchell, Former US Senate Majority Leader & Peace Envoy

Disclaimer: Although the author and publisher have made every effort to ensure that the information in this book was correct at press time, the author and publisher do not assume and hereby disclaim any liability to any party for any loss, damage, or disruption caused by errors or omissions, whether such errors or omissions result from negligence, accident, or any other cause. This book is presented solely for educational and informational purposes. The author and publisher are not offering it as legal, accounting, or other professional services advice. Neither the author nor the publisher shall be held liable or responsible to any person or entity with respect to any loss or incidental or consequential damages caused, or alleged to have been caused, directly or indirectly, by the information or advice contained herein. Every company is different and the advice and strategies contained herein may not be suitable for your situation.

With regard to General Jacoby's contribution, the author assumes responsibility for the veracity, accuracy, and source documentation of the material, including no use of classified material and conformity to copyright and usage permissions. The views expressed in the manuscript are those of the author and do not necessarily represent the official policy or position of the Department of the Army, Department of Defense, or the US government.

ISBN: 978-1-939714-15-2

Library of Congress Control Number: 2019905066

Printed in the United States of America

First Printing 2019

10 9 8 7 6 5 4 3 2 1

Interior design: AuthorScope

Distributed by Publishers Group West

Agility

HOW TO NAVIGATE THE UNKNOWN
AND SEIZE OPPORTUNITY IN A
WORLD OF DISRUPTION

To our families
for their unconditional love and support—
and for their endless patience with our attempts to be agile.

Agility

HOW TO NAVIGATE THE UNKNOWN
AND SEIZE OPPORTUNITY IN A
WORLD OF DISRUPTION

LEO M. TILMAN

GENERAL CHARLES JACOBY (RET.)

MISSIONDAY

"In the realm of the unknown, difficulties must be viewed as a hidden treasure!"

— Aleksandr Solzhenitsyn, *The First Circle*

"The first, the supreme, the most far-reaching act of judgment that the statesman and commander have to make is to establish ... the kind of war on which they are embarking; neither mistaking it for, nor trying to turn it into, something that is alien to its nature."

—Carl von Clausewitz, *On War*

CONTENTS

INTRODUCTION

In a brilliant advertising campaign from a number of years ago, a man is fishing in a rowboat on a tranquil lake surrounded by evergreens. We congratulate him for being able to take what we imagine is a well-deserved break. But then the camera zooms out, and we see that his back is turned to a massive waterfall his boat is about to plunge over. His fate is sealed; there is no way he can row away fast enough now.

Every organization today may abruptly find itself heading toward an environmental shift that poses an existential threat, a transformational opportunity, or both. The disruption across all domains is already staggering, and it's picking up speed. In this whirlwind of change, we're monitoring the developments we've deemed relevant. But are we focusing our attention on the right targets? Are we scanning the horizon broadly and vigilantly enough? Are we committing sufficient resources and taking vigorous enough action?

In business, some organizations are making bold moves, even fundamentally transformative ones. The behemoth of online advertising seems determined to become a car manufacturer and a space explorer. The pioneering designer and maker of mobile devices is offering credit cards and venturing into original entertainment content. A leading drugstore chain has bought a health insurer. A ride-sharing company is going into electric bikes. An e-commerce giant is making movies, selling groceries and managing home deliveries. In contrast, other organizations, some previously iconic, are retracing past adventures, hoping to return to traditional strengths.

A painful irony is that evolution has endowed us with traits that don't mix well with complexity and uncertainty, as such environments tend to make us risk-averse, either reluctant to act or impulsive, and focused on fending off dangers. That is why this era is testing organizational decision-making more fiercely than ever before. Should we go on the offense and seize perceived opportunities, even if it's at great risk? Or would we be better off husbanding our resources, playing defense and waiting for opponents to make a mistake? Can we possibly manage to do both?

There is one action we must take for sure, irrespective of whether we are in business, government, the military or the world of NGOs. We must acquire the knowledge and capabilities that will help us navigate the accelerating change. Because we have thus far seen only a sneak preview of what Peter Drucker called the "future that has already happened." Thanks to big-data analytics and cloud computing, we're getting better and better at assessing oceans of information in real time. Gene editing is poised to transform healthcare and agriculture. Artificial intelligence will surely change professional services, medical diagnostics and business intelligence. Equally groundbreaking developments are occurring in hypersonic systems, micro satellites, robotics, transportation, energy, 3D printing, nanotechnology, virtual and augmented reality, and distributed ledger technologies. Soon enough, we are told, our daily lives will be enveloped by the omnipresent and omniscient "internet of things." Of course, the specific manifestations of these new capabilities and the timeframes within which any of them may happen are not only unknown; they are unknowable.

The scope of the technological revolution is staggering, and yet we cannot afford to make it our sole focus. Powerful forces of geopolitical and social change are amplifying the volatility and unpredictability of our competitive environments. In today's multipolar world, established and emerging powers are aggressively vying for economic, physical and moral spheres of influence. Cyberwarfare has created entirely new kinds of adversaries, targets and vulnerabilities. The post-World War II international order and its long-standing alliances are being stressed. The fight for the hearts and minds of humanity—whose intensity is comparable to that at the height of the Cold War—is pitting democracy against authoritarianism. The battle is highlighting the stark choices between economic freedom and liberty; and between state capitalism, corporatism and free markets.

Our societies are undergoing a significant transformation of their own. Our emotions, beliefs and actions are shaped by a deafening cacophony of voices, and we often have no way of knowing their identities, qualifications or intentions. We are equally blind to the invisible hands that curate what we hear and see, with dangerous echo chambers sowing discord and division. The disregard for truth, evidence, expertise and accountability is palpable. The breakdown of trust permeates key social contracts, undermining faith in institutions fundamental to our values. Our privacy and trust have become commodities to be bought and sold.

Yet this environment of uncertainty and conflict is also one of great promise. The power of dynamic organizations that thrive on ingenuity, smart risk-taking and bold action is on full display. Opportunities abound for systemic thinkers who can shape a compelling vision for the future and empower organizations to brave the unknown intelligently. For humanity, the promise is greater prosperity in the broadest sense: inclusive economies, access to knowledge, longer and healthier lives, and brand-new avenues for self-discovery and self-actualization.

To thrive in the years ahead, all organizations, both public and private, will need to make a concerted and ongoing investment in the knowledge, capabilities, processes and cultures that foster a distinctive and all too rare organizational quality—*agility*. Only then will they be positioned to adroitly respond to change, exploit uncertainty deliberately and decisively, and seize the unprecedented possibilities of this new age.

CHAPTER 1

THE AGILITY MISSION

Agile organizations treat disruption and adversity as opportunities. They grab the initiative and turn the environment into a critical supporter of their vision. In contrast, organizations that cling to the status quo and fail to take smart risks face extinction. The disparity between those that thrive and those that stumble grows when the pace of change accelerates. According to Innosight, the average tenure of a firm on the S&P 500 index has shortened from thirty-three years in 1965 to twenty years in 1990. It's expected to continue shrinking, with some analyses indicating that nearly half of today's index may turn over in the next ten years.[1] Yet the need to prioritize learning how to confront the intensifying disruption and uncertainty is largely absent from the top-line messaging, missions and visions of the leading global companies.

Evolutionary fitness of organizations is determined by their ability to effectively respond to environmental changes. Extinctions generally follow a familiar pattern. Environmental signals—both positive and negative—are undetected or ignored. Leaders fail to recognize the new reality and accept it for what it is. No viable strategic vision for the new environment is developed. Instead, a myriad of tactical activities is deployed, without amounting to a coherent strategy. Existential risks remain hidden until it's too late.

Of course, a chorus of advice to leaders and organizations is urging them to address these challenges by becoming more nimble, adaptable, flexible, dynamic and yes, agile. But none of these terms has been rigorously defined or differentiated from one another. The absence of a cogent understanding of what's required is causing confusion and leading to incomplete or generic prescriptions. Those can be not only ineffective but outright damaging. The approach to fostering agility we introduce in this book fills the gap by providing a comprehensive intellectual framework as well as an operational roadmap. The objective is to enable all organizations to quickly recognize threats and opportunities, shape timely responses, decisively execute, and do so consistently as environments change.

So, what *is* agility? The term is used in a range of contexts. Freestyle rappers refer to mental agility, as do chess players and psychologists. Business executives pursue agile marketing and supply-chain strategies. Management consultants advocate leadership agility. Computer scientists focus on agile software development. Most commonly, though, the term is evoked in the realm of athletics, where its distinctive character is most intuitively perceived. Even those of us who are neither athletes nor fans easily appreciate the hallmarks of agility on a field or court.[2]

While sprinting requires speed, marathon running demands endurance and weightlifting entails strength, in contrast, agility is the key to being a successful football running back, a slalom skier, a tennis player or a martial artist. Agility involves both the knowledge of the competitive environment and the ability to shape and use it to our advantage. A running back reads the defense, uses his blockers and quickly changes direction based on rapidly changing threats and opportunities. A tennis player shapes a strategy and dynamically uses an arsenal of shots based on the prior knowledge of the opponent, the ongoing assessment during play and the unique circumstances of each point. In judo, a martial artist uses a variety of forces—gravity, momentum, friction—to make his opponent lose balance, thus taking advantage of both his strengths and vulnerabilities. While a sprinter, a runner or a cross-country skier may, in fact, be agile, we would not know it by watching them compete within the predictable parameters of their disciplines.

In the same way that a sprinter's speed should not be confused with agility, organizations do not demonstrate agility by flawlessly executing pre-defined strategies or mitigating known threats. The need for agility in business, government and warfare arises precisely from the uncertainty and complexity of the competitive environment. Agility requires the capacity to rigorously assess a situation and decide in a timely manner how, when, and to what end our talents and resources should be deployed. It entails the ability to dynamically deploy all of our capabilities—individually and in combination—with a most effective use of time and energy. Importantly, again as in sports, while agility is not *merely* strength, speed, power or endurance, those qualities are all necessary enablers of agility. To win through agility, we don't need to be the bigg*est*, the fast*est* or the strong*est*, but we do have to be big *enough*, strong *enough* and fast *enough*.

In operating with agility, we are dealing not only with the laws of nature but also with the laws of human nature. The human factors of leadership, culture and morality are paramount. No physical capabilities, knowledge or special talents can compensate for the lack of courage to make hard decisions or for the mistrust that undermines our ability to act as a cohesive team.

Our definition of agility and the process we present for fostering it were designed to address all of these requirements—to be comprehensive, detailing all essential components. We define agility as:

> *The organizational capacity to effectively detect, assess and respond to environmental changes in ways that are purposeful, decisive and grounded in the will to win.*

Agile organizations possess both strategic and tactical agility. Strategic agility enables entire organizations to move with the *speed of relevance*: to detect and assess major trends and environmental changes and dynamically adapt their strategic visions, business models, human capital and campaign plans.[3] Tactical agility enables employees to move with the *speed of the challenge*: to take smart risks, capture opportunities, improvise and innovate as they execute a clear strategy. This requires the buy-in and active engagement of the whole organization, up and down the hierarchy and out to the very edges. When we are agile both strategically and tactically, we can confidently brave the world of accelerating change and channel the entirety of the organization's energy toward clear, inspirational objectives.

Achieving agility may seem an ideal that is simply impossible to operationalize. But in both our personal experience and our research of organizations, we have seen it in action, to great effect. Even in the most complex of situations, with an extraordinary number of players and variables, as well as a myriad of risks, agility can be consistently achieved. Take the case of the D-Day invasion of Normandy that we'll examine in detail in the last chapter—one of the most complex strategic operations ever undertaken.

Known as Operation Overlord, the Battle of Normandy was a culmination of a multi-year strategic process that exemplifies agility. It was based on several pivotal acts of judgment about the nature of the Nazi threat; the order in which the Allies should focus on the defeat of the Axis powers—vanquishing Germany and Italy first, and then focusing fully on Japan; and the optimal method to defeat Germany, a cross-channel attack into Europe. The implementation of the strategy involved the transformation of the entire US economy into an "arsenal of democracy" and a great deal of innovation, for the war efforts in general and for the amphibious landing in Europe in particular. Shaping operations, such as North Africa and the Battle of the Atlantic, extensive training of troops, large-scale war games, collection of intelligence and comprehensive disinformation campaigns were conducted in parallel.

On the day of the invasion, most of what could go wrong did go wrong. Bad weather forced delays, strong currents pushed vessels away from targeted landing spots, paratroopers were dropped in wrong locations and widely scattered around a large area, and in spite of the disinformation campaign, beaches were well fortified by the enemy. It was tactical agility that saved the day. In response to unforeseen challenges, soldiers spontaneously formed small combat units and cohered around actions best suited to advance the overall mission. Tanks were mounted with metal "tusks" to overcome the unexpected hedgerow obstacles. Strategic bombers were repurposed as tactical air support to ground units attempting to break out of the beachheads. Real-time decentralized improvisations and smart risk-taking by soldiers and leaders were purposeful, deliberate and grounded in the will to win.

One of the central messages of this book is that organizational agility is achievable. It can be taught, learned and consistently practiced via methodical inquiry, preparation and planning. It is a *choice* followed by action and hard work. It requires a specific organizational setting, quality of knowledge and set of capabilities that must be deliberately created and relentlessly nurtured by senior leaders. The capabilities of agility become ingrained in thought processes, practices and culture only if they are positioned as essential priorities and standards of excellence—and embraced as such by the whole organization. With this purposeful and disciplined approach, agility becomes a *mindset*, a way of thinking that determines how we study environments and how we operate on a day-to-day basis. When we make the choice to become agile, adopt the agility mindset, equip ourselves with requisite knowledge and capabilities, embed agility into our processes and culture—and stay vigilant in continuously nurturing it throughout the organization—agility becomes an enduring *state of being*.

Developing the Framework for Agility

The origins of this book date back to the discovery that each of us has been thinking about organizational agility for decades. We've drawn, in part, on our differing experiences of leading and advising major organizations across the public and private spheres.

Chuck's original interest came from wrestling with the military requirements for agility. Having experienced three major US military drawdowns in his career,[4] he's witnessed the same pattern. Despite severe personnel cuts and a decimation of readiness and modernization budgets, the military's mission to protect the nation continued to broaden and become more complex. This meant doing more with less, and the answer was always the same: becoming leaner, more lethal, more efficient and, yes, more agile. The problem, of course, was that agility was never really defined; it never became a part of the operational doctrine, except in words; and it meant different things to different people. It was a buzzword cloaked in a sort of mysticism that masked unreadiness and indecision about how to purposefully approach the uncertain times. In an article published in the *Joint Force Quarterly*, Chuck and his co-author Major Ryan Shaw examined, in a military context, some of the essential attributes of a theory of agility and the qualities of an agile leader. We've drawn on that analysis.

Leo's interest in agility came from an entirely different direction. In his 2008 book *Financial Darwinism*, he introduced a way to view companies and organizations as portfolios of risks. The need was clear: traditional approaches to management and strategy—that analyzed corporate missions and visions; products and services; business lines and organizational charts; and income and balance sheet statements—were obscuring the role of risk in business models. *Financial Darwinism* argued that the *dynamism* with which the organization's portfolio of risks is managed, and the leadership practices and organizational behaviors that facilitate it, is a major determinant of performance, relevance and long-term survival. Doing this well required risk intelligence: the capacity to holistically think about risk and uncertainty when making pivotal strategic, financial and organizational decisions. The book's premise—that most organizations don't manage their portfolios of risks rigorously and dynamically enough—was validated by the mass extinctions of companies and investors during the global financial crisis of 2008–09. The concept of risk-intelligent dynamism was a precursor to our concept of agility.

While we used different languages and drew on very different experiences, the alignment of our thinking was truly striking. As we worked together on advising companies and designing new models for public/private partnerships, we kept returning to the need for a comprehensive theory of agility. Senior leaders involved in the complex global economic environment—with its rapid pace of change, unexpected disruptions and cascading second- and third-order effects—had the same challenges as top military commanders. They knew their organizations had to change and become more agile, but they didn't know precisely what that meant or how to achieve it. So, we decided to work together to deeply investigate the nature of agility and create a very practical and actionable roadmap that would enable any organization to become agile.

We structured the book to first present a compelling case that agility was urgently needed (Chapters 1 and 2)—and then make it come alive as a useful theory, operational doctrine and leadership practice. Our model was the seminal book *On War* by the Prussian general and military theorist Carl von Clausewitz. We focused on the specific reason why that book has been embraced by the western world for nearly two centuries. Clausewitz starts with inquiry into the fundamental nature of conflict. His practical guidance on how to develop strategy and conduct military operations comes later—all grounded in a rigorous understanding of the purpose, meaning and nature of war.

Similarly, we set out to carefully examine the fundamental nature of agility and explain what agility is and is not. This entailed rigorously defining agility; deconstructing it into major components (Chapter 3); and identifying the organizational competencies necessary to achieve it (Chapters 4 through 8 and Chapter 10). We felt it was also critical to describe the role of leadership and culture in creating and sustaining agility (Chapter 9). Lastly, we wanted to unify the entire book by describing how the full process operates, using two extended real-world examples from the business and military domains (Chapter 11).

As we delved into the nature and ingredients of agility, we examined a variety of historical events and organizational experiences where agility was a key determinant of success. We also studied a wealth of situations in which a lack of agility has resulted in assorted failures in government, business, finance, warfare and emergency management. Throughout the book, we provide examples that fall into three categories. One is of organizations and campaigns we have led or worked closely with (the Iraq War, Bear Stearns, Hurricane Sandy, Wachovia, US government credit programs and Freddie Mac). For others, we synthesized various sources—interviews with key decision-makers, the research of others and our own experience—to demonstrate how the prism of agility can illuminate familiar stories in new ways (the Northern Ireland Peace Process, BlackRock, General Motors, Hurricane Katrina, Putin's Russia and Goldman Sachs). Finally, we developed a set of longer and more elaborate examples to showcase the full approach in action, based on close collaboration with the leaders of organizations, to describe in detail their experiences and practices (IMAX, Western Union and leading US fire departments). For the account of the Battle of Normandy, we drew on extensive historical sources.

Our development of the framework for agility and the selection of examples were based on a few key additional considerations. First, we believed that understanding and operationalizing agility required integrating military and business theory and practice on a much deeper level than has been done to date. Second, we wanted to enrich the combined business and military insights with experiences from the worlds of government, emergency management, finance and NGOs. For example, we have melded the ways in which risk is defined and exploited—and the role that risk plays in strategy development and organizational design—across many domains.

We also realized that in order to adequately define agility and make it actionable, we had to bridge the silos that divide the literatures and practices of strategy, management, risk, leadership and culture. Elements from each are critical to fostering agility, but these fields are rarely integrated. Approaches to strategy development often don't account for the leadership, cultural and organizational factors that may significantly influence its execution. Culture and leadership discussions are often disconnected from strategy, finance and behavioral economics. The richness and rigor of modern risk management as a scientific discipline has, for the most part, been left out of mainstream books on strategy, management, leadership and culture. As we worked on this integration, we were struck by just how invaluable the contributions of military thinking are to this synthesis, offering vital guidance not only when it comes to high-stakes decision-making but across strategic, organizational and tactical spheres. For example, the US military's doctrine of Mission Command was vital in formulating a command-and-control philosophy that can be adapted to fostering agility at any organization.

The Process, the Pillars and the Setting of Agility

The Agility Process we present—designed to be rigorous, flexible and repeatable—directly reflects our definition of agility. It starts with detection of environmental changes that warrant action. Once detected, threats and opportunities are rigorously assessed, along with a range of potential responses. After the preferred course of action is determined and execution unfolds, ongoing environmental changes—including those created by our own actions—are continuously monitored and evaluated with rigor. Sometimes they lead to adjustments of strategic plans and tactics, while at other times they help determine that deliberate inaction is the right option.

Vital to an effective process for achieving agility is that it is not defined or operationalized in a rigid, one-size-fits-all way. Organizations must be able to tailor it to the nature of their business and evolving circumstances. They should be able to cultivate the capabilities that support it in advance, activate them as needed and enhance them through experience. All stages of the "detect, assess, respond" process are enabled by three essential core competencies—*risk intelligence*, *decisiveness* and *execution dexterity*—which we refer to as *pillars of agility*.

Risk Intelligence

Risk intelligence enables the organization to recognize and assess environmental changes in real time. It helps widen the usually too-narrow scope of detection, uncover hidden connections among risks, aggregate a multitude of different risks, and align risk with goals and resources. By representing organizations as dynamic portfolios of risks, it significantly enriches the prevailing methods of assessing business models and fitness.

To facilitate a continuous monitoring of the full scope of risks and uncertainties, we introduce a process we call *fighting for risk intelligence*. It involves the entire organization, out to its very edges, and has a dual objective:

1) sift through vast reams of data in order to separate relevant information from noise, and 2) obtain the information that is not readily available or that our adversaries are determined to deny us.

We next introduce the concept of a *risk radar,* which integrates a wealth of information produced by the fight for risk intelligence and paves the way to actively managing the organization's portfolio of risks. We describe in detail how a risk radar can be constructed and used in practice. This not only improves detection but assists with assessment and strategic planning, establishes a common language, and provides a mechanism for communication of environmental signals, emerging threats and opportunities all around the organization. In the process, staying vigilant, gathering intelligence and managing risk become essential elements of everyone's responsibilities.

One of our main themes is that risk should be not be viewed as just a threat that must be mitigated. Instead, we position the organization's portfolio of risks as a set of indispensable arrows in the quiver of decision makers. Risks are drivers of performance that have no inherent positive or negative connotations. Instead of "avoiding," "controlling" and "mitigating" risk, agile organizations exploit, manage and channel risk and uncertainty in pursuit of their goals.

Decisiveness

Decisiveness, which we define as a *bias for deliberate action,* is a core competence that positions organizations to act in a timely and calculated manner when opportunities and challenges arise. It is a powerful remedy against inaction and risk-aversion. Decisiveness is enabled by the organization's command-and-control philosophy, leadership and culture. Risk intelligence plays a key role as well because deliberate actions follow a fight for risk intelligence and an evidence-based inquiry and debate.

Decisiveness rests on a common understanding and a clear communication of what must be achieved and why—up and down the chain of command, from senior leaders all the way to the edges of the organization. We have drawn on the doctrine of Mission Command to develop a command-and-control approach that fosters empowerment and agility and can be tailored to any organization. Throughout, we leveraged Chuck's experience implementing it with teams on the battlefield, in preparation for war, and in peacetime operations, such as hurricane response.

As one of the generic (and dangerous) prescriptions in an era of accelerating disruption, much has been written about democratizing authority and creating flat organizations in order to foster adaptability and innovation. Mission Command is by no means a democratization of leadership or a diffusion of responsibility. The commander is the critical driver of success, establishing the strategic direction, helping visualize how an operation should unfold and empowering *disciplined* initiative.

Mission Command combines centralized, top-down vision and planning with empowered decentralized execution. Leaders at all levels are expected to exercise initiative within clearly defined boundaries, which enables them to act aggressively and independently to accomplish the mission. Building on this foundation, we introduce a framework we call *operationalized strategic vision* that enables leaders to craft and clearly communicate the organizational purpose, strategic direction, business philosophy and parameters for decision-making authority. We also demonstrate that the level of decentralization must be determined by the organization's portfolio of risks.

Execution Dexterity

Execution dexterity, the third pillar of agility, is the organizational ability to dynamically and effectively use all our resources and capabilities—individually and in combinations—in ways that are custom-tailored to the circumstances at hand. This entails being equipped with a full arsenal of capabilities, which we call levers, having developed each lever to be of adequate quality and capacity, having the mastery of each lever, and having the ability to holistically decide how, when and to what end the appropriate combinations of levers should be deployed. Execution dexterity also plays a vital role in the strategy development process, because our realism about the strengths and weaknesses of our capabilities and our ability to effectively deploy them is a critical aspect of shaping an effective strategy.

When we discuss the concept of execution dexterity with leadership teams across public and private sectors, the notion that levers of agility include strategic transactions like M&A, organizational transformations or investments in IT and infrastructure is intuitive. What often comes as a surprise is the fact that *risk* levers—the total amount of risk an organization takes in pursuit of its objectives and the structure of its portfolio of risks—are an integral part of the arsenal. They must be used holistically and in concert with more familiar business, organizational and financial tools.

The Agility Setting

Detecting, assessing and responding to change is hard work. The effective execution of all stages of the Agility Process requires a particular style of leadership that cultivates an organizational environment of trust, honesty, accountability and empowerment. We call this environment the Agility Setting. Stepping into the unknown requires courage, conviction and tolerance for setbacks and failures. All team members must be unified around a common cause and values and must be alert and engaged. They must be comfortable bearing bad news, voicing dissent and rigorously debating environmental signals and potential responses. A principled pursuit of truth must trump formal authority, ideologies and personal agendas, turning the entire organization into what we call The Forum of Truth. People at all levels need to feel both accountable and empowered to improvise and take well-calculated risks. For all of this to happen, they need to trust that their leaders and colleagues have their backs.

The Agility Setting is the product of what we call the *special brand of leadership.* Executives who possess it are easy to spot. They put forth a viable and compelling strategic vision that keeps the organization purposeful and relevant. Such leaders define, own, communicate and relentlessly nurture the culture of trust. They view themselves as de facto Chief Risk Officers, devoting a concerted effort to understanding and managing the organization's portfolio of risks. Their actions are consistent with their words, and with the organizational purpose, values and standards of behavior. They maintain intense engagement with their people, investing in authentic relationships.

This type of leadership cannot be legislated into being; it doesn't simply emerge from operational processes. It can only be fostered by example and promulgated by practice. One of the key messages of this book is that this brand of leadership can be taught, and that developing executives who exemplify it is a critical aspect of building agile organizations.

~

Our hope is that this book will empower and be of practical use to senior leaders across public and private sectors—corporate CEOs and their leadership teams, boards of directors, senior government officials, military commanders, educational administrators, institutional investors, management consultants, entrepreneurs and other executives. We also hope this book will be helpful to managers at all levels, who can implement many of the practices with their teams and cultivate agility by adopting the relevant mindset, capabilities and leadership style.

As we proceed to illuminate the framework and practices of agility, we'll begin, in the next chapter, by delving into the fundamental nature of all competitive environments. In addition to discussing some of the current trends driving change and conflict, we'll examine the key ramifications of the inherent complexity and uncertainty of our adaptive operating landscapes. We'll then fully probe the components of agility in Chapter 3.

Chapter 2

FOG, FRICTION AND THE EDGE OF CHAOS

In Tolstoy's *War and Peace*, Napoleon is portrayed receiving reports from the battlefield during the 1812 Battle of Borodino. All of them turned out to be wrong. Some accounts were inaccurate because "it was impossible in the heat of battle to say what was happening at any given moment." In some cases, the messengers didn't actually witness what they were reporting but simply related what they learned from others. Some reports had been accurate at first, but by the time they were delivered, circumstances had drastically changed.[5] Today's leaders are bound to find this state of affairs eerily familiar.

All competitive environments, with their complexities, threats and opportunities, exhibit significant parallels with military conflicts. The role of chance permeates every action and counteraction. Unexpected developments, external forces and human factors come into play. Few plans survive contact with reality because our assumptions turn out to be incorrect, our adversaries act in unforeseen ways, or because our actions set in motion a multitude of forces that change the operating landscape itself.

Clausewitz wrote that war is the "continuation of politics by other means."[6] Putting war into the larger political context points to why his famous diagnosis of warfare is so applicable well beyond the battlefield.

Clausewitz observed that any conflict situation is a realm of overarching uncertainty, shrouded in *fog* and *friction*, and this is most definitely the case with the complex business, diplomatic, political and security environments of the twenty-first century.

Fog is the informational ambiguity that envelops every dynamic environment in which players compete. In the heat of battle whether in business, government or warfare, the truth of the situation may not be fully discernable. Of course, we can and should make a concerted effort to grasp what's actually happening; uncover the intentions and capabilities of our adversaries; and develop a birds-eye view of the whole operating landscape. Yet the inherent opacity of competitive situations, and the sheer multitude of forces at play, are bound to leave us with an incomplete, and often flawed, understanding.

This task is being progressively complicated by the unique features of the modern world. Sifting through previously unimaginable amounts of data and distilling information that is relevant and reliable is increasingly challenging. New technologies are allowing rivals to attack our communication systems and deny us information about their plans and vulnerabilities ever more effectively. Meanwhile, social media has become a powerful medium for disseminating deception and propaganda, sowing societal animosity, and fostering radicalization and violence.

As for friction, it is an inherent feature of all operating environments that are intensely competitive, subject to the role of chance and ridden with adversity. Whenever we set out to make ideas and plans a reality we invariably face multifaceted manifestations of uncertainty. We encounter all manner of unexpected events and hostile actions. Technological failures, incidents and mistakes build upon each other, causing chain reactions that cannot be predicted or analyzed theoretically. A multitude of human factors comes into play, because all competitive and adversarial situations, as Clausewitz put it, are a realm of "confusion, exhaustion and fear" and a "trial" of moral, psychological and physical forces. It is friction that makes the reality of an actual battlefield different, in his words, from "war on paper."

One of our main themes is that agile organizations thrive in environments of change, ambiguity and adversity. In physics, friction is the force of resistance that can impede motion, start a fire and lead to wear or a loss of energy. But friction also creates traction, facilitating movement and enabling us to control our speed or change direction. Similarly, while the friction inherent in all competitive environments can upend our plans and impede activity and progress, it also affects our adversaries and creates situations ripe with opportunities to be exploited. Friction is a powerful ally of agility.

Accelerating Change

Thanks to intensifying disruption and conflict-ridden geopolitical and societal backdrops, the fog and friction of our competitive environments are becoming even more daunting. In describing the "scale, scope and complexity" of the ongoing Fourth Industrial Revolution, founder of the World Economic Forum Klaus Schwab forcefully conveys "the transformation... unlike anything humankind has experienced before."[7] Most industries in most countries are either in the midst of or on the verge of disruption, and "a fusion of technologies" is "blurring the lines between the physical, digital and biological spheres." The very technologies that are driving progress pose not only competitive but existential threats. Even leading experts are no longer capable of absorbing or synthesizing the full range of developments in their domains.

This technological revolution is taking place in a global setting that the US military describes as *persistent conflict*.[8] Geopolitical rivals are working hard to handicap each others' strategic interests, fracture alliances and increase instability. Nation states and non-state actors are increasingly brazen in using military force to achieve political, ideological and economic objectives. They've become masterful at using the entire arsenal of modern hybrid warfare to operate just below the threshold of violence that could ignite an armed conflict.[9]

The effort to gain competitive and national security advantages in the future is equally intense, with global competitors heavily investing in advanced technologies and military capabilities. The fight for dominance in artificial intelligence, gene editing and quantum computers is intensifying and is taking many forms: government support of critical industries, acquisition of innovative companies, access to intellectual property disguised as minority investments, industrial espionage and outright cyber theft. Concerted efforts to gain access to natural resources—with a special focus on the nexus of water, food and energy—are posing their own dangers and challenges.

Who will win the arms race of artificial intelligence and quantum computers? Will gene-edited super-intelligent "designer babies" change the course of human evolution? Will robotization eliminate billions of jobs? What happens when unmanned weapons systems start making moral judgments? What impact will the eradication of entire species of disease-carrying insects have on various ecosystems? The pervasive uncertainty surrounding such questions leads to an important realization. Relentlessly studying our adversaries and the trends that are shaping our "future that has already happened" is critically important but not sufficient. Ways in which we define and operationalize agility must explicitly reflect the full nature of our operating environments—with their inherent fog, friction and, as we'll see momentarily, complexity and a proclivity to descend into chaos.

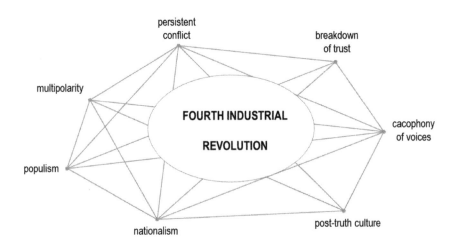

The Operating Environment

Complexity and Chaos

It's remarkable how valuable Clausewitz's prism of fog and friction still is, two hundred years later, in illuminating the nature of our operating landscapes. His insights can now be enriched by the modern multidisciplinary field that studies complex adaptive systems—from financial markets, smart cities and biological ecosystems to power grids, traffic flows and social networks.

The competitive environments for organizations of all kinds are such complex adaptive systems. They are constantly changing and evolving. They lack centralized control. They are inhabited by a multitude of stakeholders driven by distinct objectives, risk tolerances and modes of operation. These players interact in dynamic tension with one another, alternating between the urges to recoil from and engage in risk-taking and aggression. Their actions and adaptations lead to entirely unpredictable patterns and outcomes.[10] Previously irrelevant factors suddenly become exceedingly influential and vice versa.[11] Local knowledge does not lead to the understanding of the environment as a whole.

In complex adaptive systems, small actions or shocks can lead to disproportionately large consequences, and expansive and forceful actions can produce negligible results. This means that, in the words of military theorist Keith Green, we often "cannot answer credibly and convincingly whether a particular action has helped or harmed the cause." Sometimes, we can't even "answer except with anecdotal evidence or gut feeling" a seemingly "simple question: Are we winning or losing?"[12] The recent so-called quantitative easing programs by central banks are a case in point. In the aftermath of the global financial crisis of 2008–09, the US Federal Reserve deployed over two *trillion* dollars in an attempt to keep long-term interest rates low. Ten years later, as pointed out in the *Wall Street Journal,* neither central banking officials nor anyone else could articulate the impact of this program, if any, on economic growth and business activity.[13]

As part of the fight for risk intelligence, we must vigilantly watch for the factors that have potential to affect the functioning of our operating environments. For example, the impact of social media on everything from the organization of civil protests and emergency responses to catastrophes to the reputations of both individuals and businesses emerged by stealth. The dynamics of financial markets have been radically transformed by the virtually instantaneous transmission of geopolitical, economic and company-specific news.

Even when our complex adaptive habitats appear to be balanced and tranquil, they are, in the words of historian Niall Ferguson, constantly "teetering on the edge of chaos."[14] They experience bouts of extreme volatility. An unpredictable action or shock can send the entire economic, financial or geopolitical system into a state of a "radical disequilibrium" and change. These so-called phase transitions can develop either gradually or abruptly. They can be catalyzed by external forces, such as the Brexit referendum in 2016 or Russia's sovereign debt default in 1998. They can also result from the long-standing pressures within a system reaching a tipping point. The surge of the #MeToo Movement in 2017 is exemplary.[15]

In the words of military historians David Keithly and Stephen Ferris, fog and friction "remain as resistant to technological fixes as the common cold has to the march of modern medicine."[16] Just as advances in risk management haven't ridded the global financial system of shocks and crises, attempts to mechanically use new technologies to whisk away uncertainty or cut through the complexity are bound to be ineffective or even self-defeating.

We designed the Agility Process to enable constant monitoring of our operating landscapes and dynamic adjustments of tactics and strategies out of recognition that fog, friction, complexity, chaos and intensifying change are part of our permanent reality. This understanding must be explicitly reflected in how we foster situational awareness, manage portfolios of risks, develop new capabilities, and shape mindsets and cultures. In the latter regard, since organizational agility is a human-driven response to change, the vagaries of the innate human responses to risk and uncertainty must be recognized and dealt with head-on.

The Antitheses of Agility

Change, fog, and friction can be paralyzing. This phenomenon—long known to leaders and behavioral economists alike—has deep evolutionary origins, leading to the familiar organizational behavior we refer to as a *bias for inaction*. As Nobel Prize winning psychologist Daniel Kahneman writes, "organisms that treat threats as more urgent than opportunities have a better chance" of survival.[17] As a result, in our personal and professional lives we naturally prioritize "bad news;" our fear of failing "to reach a goal is much stronger than the desire to exceed it." In his Prospect Theory, co-authored with Amos Tversky, and subsequent studies of human biases, Kahneman points to these evolutionary forces to explain why we view potential disadvantages of change more negatively than its advantages.[18] Moreover, he notes, our aversion to losses and failures spikes when stakes are high, and we have stronger emotional reactions to the outcomes produced by our actions than the same outcomes if they result from inaction.

In the presence of uncertainty, all of this makes us innately reluctant to make decisions that could lead to loss or regret. There is never a shortage of perfectly sensible excuses for not making a decision or delaying action, which often compels us to kick the can down the road or resort to uninspired and risk-averse choices. Other factors—such as a lack of strategic vision, diffusion of authority and responsibility, or misaligned incentives—tend to make matters worse. Even when we effectively detect and assess change, our response may be delayed—or even prevented—by, again in Kahneman's words, a powerful "gravitational force" that favors the "status quo."

Modern behavioral economics is aligned with Clausewitz's diagnosis that indecision is "native to the human mind," making inactivity "the rule" and progress "the exception." Inaction is, of course, antithetical to agility. This is true not only because it hampers effective responses to threats and opportunities, but also because it yields the initiative to others, often putting us on the defensive. To recognize and pre-empt these ills of inaction, President Theodore Roosevelt once observed that "in any moment of decision, the best thing you can do is the right thing, the next best thing is the wrong thing, and the worst thing you can do is nothing." This statement should be taken with a grain of salt because certain "wrong things"—half-baked decisions driven by gut reactions and unwarranted optimism—can be lethal.

In deconstructing agility, we make an important distinction between a bias for inaction and *deliberate inaction* based on rigorous decision-making grounded in the understanding of risk. Such well-considered inaction can be invaluable, giving us an opportunity to gather additional intelligence, deepen trust, and improve capabilities and preparedness. Then we can decisively strike when the time is right. From this perspective, deliberate inaction is an integral part of organizational decisiveness.

In addition to inaction and poorly conceived reactions, fog and friction can lead to other destructive organizational behaviors incompatible with agility. Chief among them is micromanagement. Delegating authority requires confidence in people and tolerance for honest mistakes and failures. When leaders become overly risk-averse in the face of uncertainty, they often excessively centralize decision-making and execution authority, which deprives organizations of agility and decimates engagement and trust. This phenomenon can be exacerbated by advances in surveillance and communication technology that may create an illusion that the fog of battle can be effectively penetrated from the comfort of an executive office.

Of course, knowing when to act and when to further prepare, assessing how much risk we should take and of what kinds, and formulating a clear strategy reflective of the prevailing environment are formidable challenges. This is precisely why courageous organizational responses to change are so inspiring. In developing our framework for agility, we have, in fact, found a number of impressive examples that offer valuable insights.

The Reinvention of IMAX

A company that mesmerizes millions of movie fans around the world with larger-than-life imagery of *Star Wars, Avatar, Dunkirk* and Marvel superheroes. A winner of an Academy Award for scientific achievement. A creator of a unique medium that helps leading filmmakers realize artistic vision. One of the most recognizable global brands with over $1 billion in annual box office sales across 1,300 screens in 75 countries. Over the past 50 years, IMAX has come a long way, owing its success to a bold vision, innovation and agility.

Founded in 1967 in Canada, the company initially produced nature documentaries for museums and aquariums. Innovation was a hallmark from the start. Making groundbreaking use of multiple 35mm projectors, IMAX created stunning visual experiences. In 1970, it developed a whole new 65mm high-resolution camera along with a 70mm rolling loop projection system, which allowed for truly majestic cinematographic artistry and a uniquely powerful audience experience.

IMAX sought to break into the mainstream entertainment business, but it faced many challenges. Filmmakers had to adapt to using cameras the size of a small fridge. Theaters had to be redesigned to accommodate the equipment, which cost millions of dollars. Exhibitors had to learn to operate the massive projectors, so cumbersome that they required forklifts for installation. Contributing to the challenges was the company's business model. Exhibitors had to bear the expense of redesigning movie theaters. Additionally, they had to make an upfront payment to license IMAX's system. By shifting the upfront expense to business partners, IMAX mitigated its risk and reduced its capital needs but received only a modest percentage of box office receipts as a result.

Meanwhile, very few films were produced in the IMAX format, none of which were major releases directed at the mainstream audience. Hollywood production companies, which thrive on risk-taking when it comes to making movies, are notoriously risk-averse with respect to disruptive newcomers. They found IMAX's value proposition unclear and potentially threatening. IMAX had run into the proverbial chicken-and-egg problem. Content producers required a sufficient number of screens to show their films, while theaters needed blockbuster content to justify the investment the IMAX system required. As a result, for almost twenty years, IMAX was constrained to a niche market.

When Richard Gelfond and Brad Wechsler acquired the company through a leveraged buyout in 1994, they strongly believed that the future of

IMAX was inextricably tied to Hollywood. The central premise of their strategy for growing the business was that they could unleash the cultural and economic power of having the biggest commercial films displayed in IMAX. They knew that was going to take both technical innovation and, just as importantly, the ability to break into a very insular Hollywood ecosystem.[19]

When *Toy Story*, the first full-length computer graphics (CG) feature film, was released in 1995, IMAX technology experts noted that while the movie was shown on the conventional systems in 2D, it was actually made with 3D geometry. That meant the data existed in the files for the film to be shown in 3D on IMAX screens. The maker of *Toy Story*, Pixar, and IMAX discussed the idea of making a version of the movie for IMAX screens, and some sample shots were screen tested, but Pixar decided the CG programming didn't have adequate quality at the size of the IMAX screen.[20] The IMAX team had seen the potential, though, and continued to work on the technology. The company made its own film, *Cyberworld*, which included CG scenes rendered in 3D and showed how good CG could look on IMAX screens. That ushered in a whole new era of 3D movies. Richard Gelfond likes to describe this episode as emblematic of the company's mindset and culture. It was a sign of things to come.

But before the release of *Cyberworld*, which came out in 2000, IMAX's upward momentum was severely challenged. In 1999, the firm's stock was downgraded due to concerns over the viability of its business model, and the stock price dropped 30 percent in a single day. The owners began looking to sell the company, but declining earnings kept buyers at bay. The whole US movie theater business was facing a crisis. Audiences were dwindling and many theaters filed for bankruptcy. IMAX's earnings plunged, and its lower earnings guidance to the market instantly sent the stock tumbling again, this time 70 percent. Attempts to sell the company were abandoned. By 2001, the stock price, which had reached $40 two years earlier, dropped to 55 cents. A year later, IMAX's cash on hand was less than $10 million and $250 million in debt payments were due in the following eighteen months. The company went on life support, kept solvent thanks only to some small settlements from terminated theater deals.

In the face of this existential crisis, the senior leadership had a far-reaching realization: the firm's survival—not to mention its ability to break into the global movie industry—required a decisive foray into the digital world. The writing was on the wall. Rapidly advancing digital movie technology was bound to challenge the viability of traditional film systems. IMAX's competitors were actively working on digital solutions for cinemas that would allow films to be delivered on hard drives (no forklifts required). Gelfond and Wechsler understood that to survive, IMAX was going to have to find a way to provide cash-strapped exhibitors with a less capital-intensive way of using IMAX technology, and they saw that digital was the answer. Reengineering the IMAX system from analog to digital would allow the company to lower not only the cost of the IMAX projector but the expense of film prints.

For some companies, this process could have ended up as a defensive adaptation. After seeing an environmental change, IMAX could have acquired requisite capabilities and entered "red ocean" of increasingly commoditized products, a term introduced by W. Chan Kim and Renée Mauborgne in their *Blue Ocean Strategy.*[21] With only a marginal differentiation relative to its competitors, the firm could have tried to compete by doing things more efficiently and cheaply. IMAX had no interest in such an outcome.

The company decisively moved to enter the digital marketplace as a major player, completely revamping its technology, all without vast R&D and human resources. But that was not enough. IMAX needed much more content to offer theaters, and it needed to get it quickly. Yet there were no ways to convert existing Hollywood blockbusters to the IMAX format. In fact, the attempts to do so revealed that when a film image was enlarged, all imperfections became glaringly visible, negating all the visual advantages of an IMAX system.

To overcome this seemingly intractable challenge, in 2002 IMAX invented a groundbreaking process for remastering Hollywood films. This process, which became known as *digital remastering,* entailed scanning the content filmed with a normal camera at the highest possible resolution and then removing all visual artifacts and noise, frame by frame. Subsequently, proprietary algorithms coupled with the creative human element were used to optimize each image for the IMAX system. As a result, movies were not just enlarged and cleaned up for bigger screens but transformed. They became newly visually stunning. In parallel, the company put soundtrack technology through a sweeping makeover of its own, making sound crisper, brighter and more emotionally attuned to the stories on screen.

The invention of digital remastering enabled IMAX to shape a Blue Ocean strategy and fundamentally redefine its relevance to the key segments of the entertainment industry. The strategy paid off. These technological advances were enormously attractive to the mainstream Hollywood production companies. IMAX began to work closely with directors and producers throughout the process of making new films: helping plan shots, re-mix soundtracks and adjust virtually every frame. Audiences were willing to pay a premium for the sense of awe and adventure of these IMAX versions of movies, and with increasing numbers of hits available in the format, movie theaters could afford to dedicate resources to adopting the IMAX system.

To advance its vision of growth and redefine its relevance to the key stakeholder groups, IMAX also embarked on a business model transformation that altered its relationship with exhibitors. Rather than charge a significant upfront licensing fee, the company transitioned to a joint venture model: it provided its system for free in exchange for receiving a much larger percentage of the box office receipts. With the much greater commercial potential of IMAX movies, the company's analysis determined that there was a large upside to taking on this greater risk. The new joint venture model proved to be a win-win, helping theaters upgrade with much lower capital outlays and bring in an incremental attendance. As a result, more theaters installed IMAX systems, more movies were created in the IMAX format, and larger, enthusiastic audiences led to a greater box office success.

Yet IMAX continued to face serious threats. Several competitors reverse-engineered the IMAX system and then sued the company under anti-trust laws. In 2006, after prevailing in the lawsuits, the company put itself up for sale only to discover the absence of bidders: doubts about its viability persisted. Just when a sale auction collapsed, the US and Canadian regulators launched investigations into IMAX's accounting practices. While the company was eventually vindicated, accounting probes led to class action lawsuits. After another stock price collapse below $2, IMAX had to combat an aggressive attempt by an activist investor to acquire the company's debt and enact a hostile takeover. In recent years, a theft of IMAX's intellectual property resulted in the emergence of a major international competitor, while a well-known American company developed its own premium laser system and formed a partnership with large distributor chains.

Through all of this, the company nonetheless continued to innovate and pursue its vision and strategy in stride. The release of *Avatar* in 2009, with its unprecedented technological artistry, made the biggest splash and was the company's true coming-of-age moment as a major entertainment industry player.

An organization's ability to treat potentially existential threats and challenges as opportunities is a hallmark of agility. Amidst rapid technological change and adversity, IMAX's executives transitioned the company to a digital infrastructure, transformed its business model and redefined its relevance to key stakeholder groups. In parallel, the firm expanded into international film markets, making its Chinese network rival that in North America. In order to make strategy and execution adjustments in real time, IMAX also put in place a command-and-control center that monitors the performance and content of its 1,300 screens in 75 countries. These pivotal top-down decisions were a manifestation of strategic agility.

Realizing IMAX's vision—to create a new kind of immersive entertainment and become a key entertainment industry player—required a specific organizational setting. The entire company needed to be unified around a shared cause and a clearly articulated business philosophy. Environmental changes needed to be comprehensively assessed and parlayed into action plans. Experimentation, openness to new ideas and tolerance for mistakes needed to become a part of the cultural fabric. Adopting new technologies and entering new markets required preparedness, decisiveness and multifaceted execution capabilities.

This brings us to a fundamental point: when strategic agility is coupled with a culture of trust, empowerment and calculated risk-taking, it gives rise to tactical agility. In the case of IMAX, unforeseen challenges and opportunities that emerged during the strategy execution were detected, assessed and capitalized on through groundbreaking *bottom-up* innovation. In addition to inventing digital remastering and transforming 3D filmmaking, the company produced hundreds of innovations, large and small, including the development of the dual-projector digital system in 2008 and the next-generation laser technology system in 2013.

What makes the IMAX story especially relevant to our book is the fact that the company steadfastly pursued its disruptive strategy and produced remarkable new technologies in an environment that can be described only as a merciless battlefield enveloped in fog and friction and filled with aggressive adversaries. Yet, importantly, even when forced to focus on the defense, IMAX kept innovating, enhancing its business model and redefining its relevance to customers and partners. By doing so, it demonstrated ultimate purposefulness and the will to win that not only allowed it to survive, but also prepared it to go back on the offense when the time was right.

Codifying a Theory

When we encounter examples of organizations that successfully discern and boldly respond to change, capitalize on opportunities and withstand adversity, we cannot help but ask:

1. *Are these experiences repeatable?* In other words, have the qualities, capabilities and processes that led to past victories become so embedded in the organizational fabric that responses to future environmental shifts would be equally deliberate and effective?

2. *Can agility be rigorously defined and deconstructed?* If so, we can develop a common understanding, language and a process for cultivating agility at any organization. This process can leverage the rich experience and best ideas from different domains, such as NGOs, education, business, warfare and government.

3. *Can this capacity be learned and institutionalized through specific practices and characteristics of leadership?* If so, leaders and organizations will be able to make a choice to become agile and invest in the requisite knowledge, capabilities and cultures.

Answering these questions requires intellectual and operational clarity about what agility means and what it takes for an organization to be consistently agile. As we alluded to before, such clarity has been absent in the business realm, as illustrated by generic prescriptions, such as decentralization, and the confusion between agility, adaptability, speed and other competencies. But the lack of clarity has by no means been confined to the domain of business. As Chuck had observed, even though agility was prioritized by all military branches in one way or another, it hadn't been rigorously defined or operationalized.[22] In fact, multidisciplinary research has revealed an absence of "scientifically acceptable" metrics or even a consensus on what it takes to "recognize an altered situation that requires a change in response" and develop leaders and organizations who can do so effectively and consistently.[23]

In thinking deeply about the nature and character of war, Clausewitz was guided by the belief that "the primary purpose of any theory is to clarify concepts and ideas that have become…confused and entangled." To be practically useful—in his words, "of real service"—a theory needed to reflect the reality, be applicable across many environments and over time, and be conducive to being enhanced through experience. It couldn't be overly prescriptive, rather serving as "aid to judgment" when the unique circumstances of each situation are considered. We were guided by the same set of principles, hoping to create a theory of agility that would serve as a companion to Clausewitz's theory of conflict.

~

In the next chapter, we will more deeply probe the nature of agility and further explain why we defined it as we have. This will set the stage for further examination of the three pillars of agility, its moral and cultural setting and ultimately the process that makes agility achievable and repeatable.

CHAPTER 3

THE ESSENCE OF AGILITY

Agility enables organizations to quickly recognize change, adroitly shift priorities and resources, exploit uncertainty deliberately and decisively, and do so faster and better than their rivals. Instead of relying on superior inborn reflexes, agility is achieved through methodical inquiry, preparation and planning. It is supported by specific organizational competencies, processes and culture. Our goal in this chapter is to deconstruct the concept of agility and explore in more depth the essential components that must come together to foster and sustain this distinctive quality. Recall that we define agility as:

> *The organizational capacity to effectively detect, assess and respond to environmental changes in ways that are purposeful, decisive and grounded in the will to win.*

Effective Detection

The organizational ability to detect environmental changes that warrant a response requires a deep understanding of the competitive landscape in all its richness and complexity. To gain this awareness, we must acquire the requisite knowledge that will allow us to monitor the dominant technological, geopolitical and societal trends. We must fight for risk intelligence to uncover the intentions and vulnerabilities of our adversaries—all while studying our internal organizational environments just as deeply. We must recognize and proactively account for the inherent nature of our complex and adaptive habitat. All of this will enable us to properly interpret relevant developments and environmental signals.

Instituting a robust organization-wide detection process is challenging, and it's made more so by the pressing challenges of the day-to-day execution. Endless meetings must be attended, sales quotas must be met, emails demand quick response. Perseverance in keeping up with these demands is often viewed as a major driver of personal and organizational success. So, organizations tend to concentrate intensively on these short-term demands and their attendant risks. Stepping back to think deeply about the nature of our environment, broadening and deepening our field of vision, and sharply questioning what we do and don't know is often viewed as a luxury. Adopting the agility mindset fundamentally transforms this perspective, turning a nice-to-have "luxury" into a mission-critical priority.

The involvement of the entire organization in the detection process is critical because, as leadership expert Hal Gregersen keenly observes, "when a dramatic shift is on the horizon, the first indications usually appear in ambiguous events on the fringes of the market."[24] Agility requires that those early, weak signals involving both threats and opportunities are promptly detected and communicated to the relevant decision-makers. Keen situational awareness, astute local knowledge, and groundbreaking innovations often come from the very edges of the organization. A concerted and ongoing organization-wide effort is required to ensure that our focus on the routine and the near-term does not prevent us from reacting to a threat or an opportunity that might arise in unexpected form.

The corporate cliché "skate to where the puck is going," overly familiar as it is, helps illustrate a point fundamental to the understanding of agility: productive and timely responses to environmental changes involve *detection* rather than *prediction*. In fact, we cannot reliably forecast where the puck is going before it is passed—and trying to do so would expose us to the risk of being at the wrong place at the wrong time. The well-documented failures of human attempts at prediction speak volumes about both their futility and their dangers. The underwhelming track record of economists, equity analysts, political commentators and the so-called futurists should not be surprising. Because of the inherent opacity and uncertainty of our operating environments, future events and their likelihoods are unknowable.

Yogi Berra once famously observed that it's "tough to make predictions, especially about the future." Agile organizations take this premise to heart, abandoning prediction in favor of rigorous planning and detection. While we can't reliably predict where the puck is going in advance of a shot, we can develop a playbook of potential responses to various possibilities through extensive preparation and practice with our team. We can also learn how our teammates tend to react to certain situations so we can account for that in our plans. All of this advance work would enable us to sense—in a split second—that the puck is being passed, quickly assess its likely path and dash in that direction.

A good case in point is BlackRock's 2009 acquisition of Barclays Global Investors, a leading manager of exchange-traded funds at the time. The transaction was not based on some prediction of the future of finance; it was a response to an emerging trend—a rapidly increasing use of index investing by individual and institutional investors. The puck was already decisively moving that way, and BlackRock effectively positioned itself to become a dominant player in the space.[25] It's worth noting the surge in investor demand for index funds and away from traditional active asset management was fueled precisely by the demonstratively poor ability of asset managers to consistently predict which stocks and bonds will beat the market.

Another case of astute detection, which we'll examine more fully later, involved the peace process in Northern Ireland. When Senator George Mitchell was appointed in 1995 to lead a new round of negotiations, he embarked on a multifaceted fight for risk intelligence. Intense diplomacy went hand in hand with continuous monitoring and reassessment of new developments. Three environmental changes, unpredictable at the outset, proved pivotal in paving the way to a peace agreement.

Later in the book, we will comprehensively discuss the process of detection necessary for agility. We will cover conceptual issues, such as how to understand multifaceted drivers and consequences of different risks, and how to define risk intelligence as a core organizational competence. We will also introduce practical solutions to conducting the fight for risk intelligence and constructing risk radars. They expand on the typical organizational practices of monitoring a core set of select risks—some near-term and some significant or even existential—to provide a more comprehensive view of the complex adversarial environment.

Effective Assessment

For the process of detection to be effective, senior leaders must continually assess and explain to the whole of the organization what information is needed to shape strategy, manage risk and direct execution. In addition to describing what's relevant for decision-making, executives must also encourage everyone to look for the surprising or unexpected. In turn, professionals up and down the command chain need to use their expertise and local knowledge to educate their leaders on the meaning and potential implications of relevant new developments and environmental signals. Once potential risks and opportunities have been spotted, the quality, reliability and completeness of the information must be carefully studied. More often than not, this process will identify additional information that must be proactively collected, prompting an evaluation of the risks involved and the commitment of appropriate resources.

To be meaningful and practically useful, the environmental changes that have been detected must be placed in our unique organizational context. This requires that the entire set of risks inherent in our business model is identified and aggregated in ways that are both rigorous and intuitive. The risk radar tool we introduce provides an example of how this can be implemented in practice, allowing leaders to synthesize vast amounts of external and internal information and continuously monitor, assess, manage and govern the organization's portfolio of risks. As a result, the problem of strategic decision-making and day-to-day operations being largely disconnected from the intelligence gathered can be overcome.

Having developed situational awareness, we move on to the next stage of assessment: a forward-looking decision-making framework that we call *strategic calculus*. This method of shaping and evaluating alternatives aligns objectives with our appetite for risk. Vitally, it factors in not only our financial and operational capacity but also the psychological ability to withstand losses, overcome challenges and successfully execute. This framework can be adapted to strategic and tactical decisions and institutionalized at all organizational levels.

Later in the book, we'll discuss how Goldman Sachs successfully navigated the global financial crisis of 2008–09 by using an impressive arsenal of tools. Throughout, effective detection and assessment played an important role. As significant vulnerabilities built up in the US housing market, they were effectively recognized by both Goldman Sachs' senior leaders and those at the edges of the organization—from their own unique vantage points. As the crisis progressed, environmental signals were continually monitored, communicated and evaluated. Because the company had developed a capacity to comprehensively assess and monitor the firm-wide portfolio of risks in real time, it was able to chart a dynamic path to safety. In the words of one of the firm's senior executives, "the granular risk focus of the entire leadership team was the differentiating factor."

Contrast that agility to the failure of situational awareness and risk assessment that led to the tragic demise of Space Shuttle Columbia. On its returning fight on February 1, 2003, when the shuttle re-entered the Earth's atmosphere, it broke apart, killing all seven astronauts on board. The breakup was due to damage caused by a piece of foam insulation that had separated from the fuel tank during the launch and hit the edge of the shuttle's wing. Although it was detected that this piece was much larger than those observed during the prior flights, the risk posed to the shuttle was deemed quite low and "acceptable." Some engineers warned that the damage done might have been more substantial, but their concerns were dismissed. Investigation of the disaster determined that the shuttle's wing had indeed been ruptured by the foam, which allowed the intensely hot atmosphere to penetrate, leading to the breakup.

These examples highlight that while risk intelligence is critical to both detection and assessment, so is the Agility Setting. This organizational environment, in which evidence and solutions are rigorously analyzed and intensely debated, helps pierce through the fog of ambiguity and prevent the pressures of friction from distorting judgment. It also helps combat the powerful cognitive biases well documented by behavioral economists. Relevant ones here include our tendency to focus on information that supports our views and downplay contradictory data; to underestimate the role of chance; and to underestimate or ignore threats viewed as beyond our control. Vigorous debate also reduces the risk that convincing but flawed assessments and predictions of the future will make their way into strategic plans, economic projections and market analyses.

Effective Response

When introducing the concepts of strategic and tactical agility in Chapter 1, we described two types of organizational responses to change. The first category—the purview of the senior leaders—involves overarching adjustments in strategy, business model and balance sheet in response to major environmental disruptions. The second category encompasses smart risk-taking, innovation and improvisation by empowered employees—the tactical responses to environmental changes and friction encountered during strategy execution. Both types of responses are enabled by an ongoing monitoring and evaluation of the operating landscape. They both leverage the full power of execution dexterity, with the right combinations of business, organizational, and risk levers dynamically employed to deal with each unique situation. The following example of tactical agility illustrates how surveillance, assessment and response go hand in hand, enriching and empowering one another and leading to a continuous refinement of execution strategies.

When a long-time client, a leading financial institution, found itself under a cyberattack, it quickly discovered previously unknown vulnerabilities.[26] While the controls and protections surrounding this company's computer networks proved effective, those of some of its customers turned out to be extremely exposed, leading to a surge of fraudulent wire transfer requests. After quickly detecting the problem and mobilizing resources, our client instituted new communication and compliance protocols and fortified approval processes, thus mitigating further financial and reputational consequences. Throughout, we all watched in real time how the cyber attackers' methods mutated in an attempt to uncover additional vulnerabilities and circumvent the new protection mechanisms. Thanks to a continuous process that exemplifies tactical agility, these rapidly-evolving and escalating attacks were thwarted.

Surveillance, assessment, and response, which inform and empower one another, go hand in hand on the strategic level as well. Sometimes, as in the IMAX example, environmental changes warrant a reassessment of strategic objectives and tolerance for risk. When the shifts in the operating landscape are especially profound, senior leaders may even need to step back and holistically tackle the existential questions dealing with the very purpose of the organization and the nature of its business. Some of the drastic business transformations driven by the Fourth Industrial Revolution that we alluded to in the Introduction and describe more fully in Chapter 5 fall into this category.

Purposefulness and Decisiveness

Cohesion and a unity of effort are integral to agility. Organizations achieve them when everyone up and down the chain of command and all the way to the very edges of the organization knows what must be achieved but also why. The "what" is the organization's strategic vision—shaped, visualized and clearly communicated by the senior leaders. The "why" is an explicit expression of the organization's purpose, its overarching reason for being. The two come together in the context of the organization's values and standards. Of course, the importance of this trinity—purpose, vision and values—is a familiar theme, but our focus here is on how they facilitate agility.

As we face fog and friction and try to outmaneuver competitors, having a strategic and moral compass ensures that we don't lose sight of the overarching goals, the stakeholders we serve and the values that define us. A strong sense of purpose fosters cohesion by instilling a belief that everyone shares the risk and is working toward the same ends. It activates deeply seated human motivations by making everyone feel proud and fulfilled that their work creates something of real value to others. When combined with empowerment, this unleashes engagement, initiative and critical thinking essential to agility.

As for organizational decisiveness, it stands for a resolute willingness and ability to make decisions and execute in stride. It is fueled by purposefulness and, equally important, by intentionality and risk intelligence. That is why we define decisiveness as not just a bias for action, a term commonly used by the US military, but a bias for deliberate action.

The special brand of leadership and a culture of trust play a key role in cultivating decisiveness. At all times, senior leaders must be confident that they will receive timely and unvarnished information and advice. Subordinates all up and down the chain of command must believe that ideas, dissent and hard truths will be not only welcomed but applauded. They must trust that honest mistakes, intended for the collective best interest, will be judged in good faith. As we'll discuss more fully in Chapters 7 through 9, when this cultural environment is combined with the command-and-control doctrine and organizational design conducive to agility, our team members gain confidence to aggressively, creatively and independently pursue the mission, even if circumstances change and plans fall apart.

When Chuck was appointed Commander of United States Northern Command in 2011, he worked closely with the Department of Defense, FEMA and state and local governments to put in place the command-and-control practices, capabilities and protocols to correct for the problems behind the unfortunate government response, at all levels, to Hurricane Katrina in 2005. As a result, the unity of effort and a bias for deliberate action were prominently on display during Hurricane Sandy in 2012. Gathering and sharing information were declared a mission-critical priority right from the start, leading to comprehensive situational awareness. Mutual accountability, purposefulness stemming from clearly understood common goals and decisiveness, both strategic and tactical, paved the way to a successful response.

Will to Win

Reactive organizational adaptations are borne out of necessity. They are often initiated when a change in the operating landscape is already well under way. They are generally directed at preserving the status quo and mitigating threats, often causing organizational lethargy and pushback. As Clausewitz keenly observed, it is always "easier to hold ground than take it." However, in an environment of intensifying change and aggressive adversaries, a predominantly defensive mode of operation can cause organizations to forgo opportunities, jeopardizing long-term viability.

In most domains, to avoid losing we must have a determined resolve to win. This means we must be aggressively forward-looking, with a bias for deliberate action fueled not only by values and expectations but also by the intense desire to prevail. The capacity to overcome adversity with determination, perseverance and cohesion is absolutely necessary, but it's not sufficient. Agility requires a mindset and culture grounded in the *will to win* that encompasses what we call a *bias toward offense*.

Organizations that exemplify a bias toward offense treat change and adversity as opportunities. They proactively shape and leverage the environment to advance their objectives. They put team members up and down the command chain into a strategic thinking mode, helping ensure the organization doesn't get bogged down in the day-to-day challenges of tactical execution. They commit resources to continually strengthening situational awareness, knowledge and capabilities. In favorable environments, they seize the initiative and keep adversaries off-balance and on the defense, as illustrated by a number of examples throughout the book, including the case study of Putin's Russia in Chapter 10.

In some circumstances, of course, a defensive posture is warranted. But in such cases, a bias toward offense is equally critical, because it turns defensive measures into what Clausewitz called a "shield made up of well-directed blows." This form of defense is not preoccupied only with protecting against threats, it also entails proactive steps that prepare us to go back on the offense. In warfare, this may include efforts to weaken the enemy, such as launching carefully orchestrated counterattacks, or putting lives and assets on the line to fight for risk intelligence and plan a larger-scale attack. In business, this may involve bringing in new staff, conducting competitive intelligence analyses and allocating capital to R&D efforts to pave the way to relevant new products and services down the road. Throughout, while fending off threats, we are creating the conditions for resuming the offense when the time is right. Such ability to seamlessly and dynamically switch between defense and offense based on the circumstances at hand is a hallmark of agility.

The terms "winning" and "the will to win" are a part of the standard business and military lexicon, reflecting the zero-sum-game nature of many competitive settings. It is important to acknowledge, however, that healthcare and educational organizations, government agencies and NGOs may not have direct competitors or may not perceive themselves as in the business of "winning." And yet, in reality, these organizations do operate in competitive evolutionary environments. Just like businesses and armed forces, they are enveloped in the fog of informational ambiguity. They are continually fighting friction and inertia. Their value propositions and survival may become threatened by geopolitical, economic and societal forces. They are engaged in an intense competition for monetary resources, human talent, mind shares and relevance. They also, therefore, greatly benefit from the will to win, with their own definition of winning being aligned with the organization's overarching purpose and strategic vision.

In fact, winning must be defined as such for all types of organizations. For not-for-profit and government entities, it may encompass mission-driven goals, public policy success, societal or environmental impact, or influence. In business, winning must reflect not only near-term financial performance and competitive superiority but also an enduring relevance to all stakeholders: customers, shareholders, business partners, employees, communities and society at large. If the concept of winning is grounded in short-termism or disproportionately favors some stakeholder groups at the expense of others, agility is undermined, internal and external trust is eroded, and organizations become exposed to existential risks.

Purposefulness, decisiveness and the will to win are distinctive attributes of agility that differentiate it from adaptability and other forms of defensive reactiveness, which are the topic of the next section.

In Contrast to Agility

Having carefully deconstructed the components of agility, we can now see clearly how different this quality is from the set of related organizational traits it is often conflated with. Some discussion of each of these concepts, and how they differ from agility, is in order.

"Adaptability" is the ability to adjust or alter oneself to changed conditions—by learning from experience and improving one's fitness as a competitor.[27] While adaptability can apply to both mitigating threats and capturing opportunities, its connotation is usually reactive and defensive. In the language of the military, adaptability is a form of counter-punching that keeps strategic and operational advantage in the hands of competitors, markets or fate. Of special relevance to our book is the fact that the concept of adaptability appears to lack a strategic or moral anchor: the notion that while changing and evolving our organization should remain committed to its overarching purpose, strategy and values is missing. In short, adaptability is not purposeful or grounded in the will to win. It also does not seem to account for situations where the best way to respond to change is not by altering ourselves but by deploying an arsenal of skills and capabilities cultivated in advance, some of which may have been dormant or irrelevant in the old environment.

"Resilience" represents the organizational ability to recover from deformation caused by adversity or change.[28] This quality is an essential requirement for survival, superior performance and sustained agility. To us, resilience is a defensive capacity to maintain an organization's center of gravity—its purpose, workforce, assets, culture and capabilities—when under attack or pressure. As we will demonstrate later, resilience is an outcome of agility across two different classes of events. When environmental changes give us adequate time to react, resilience is created by the process of detection, assessment and response. For "instantaneous" adverse events—shocks that deprive an organization of the time to react or the control over events—resilience stems from the mitigation of potentially lethal risks *in advance*, which is also an aspect of agility.

Flexibility is the capacity to bend without breaking, to be modified, to yield to influence, to be willing to change or compromise.[29] When used in describing organizations, flexibility tends to refer to certain aspects of both adaptability and resilience.

Dynamism is the quality of fostering and maintaining vigorous activity and progress.[30] In business parlance, dynamic organizations are nimble, energetic and innovative. Their employees are engaged and creative. And yet, as we have all observed in practice, organizational dynamism does not necessarily lead to superior performance, situational awareness, adaptability or resilience. Dynamic organizations can lack cohesion and a unity of effort. Their cultures can disintegrate under pressure. They may possess tactical agility but lack strategic agility, making them especially vulnerable to dramatic environmental changes that warrant significant adjustments of vision and strategy.

Antifragility—a term introduced by Nassim Nicholas Taleb—stands for a capacity to benefit from disorder. To be antifragile, an entity must be risk-intelligent and resilient: able to assess and mitigate especially dangerous risks. Beyond survival, antifragility entails a deliberate exploitation of uncertainty: taking unrelated risks that have a limited downside and a significant upside. This includes, for example, innovating through tinkering, making venture-capital investments or betting on the fact that fragile players and systems will eventually collapse. Interestingly, while antifragile entities do benefit from disorder, they do so in ways that are fairly static: exposing themselves to a carefully constructed set of promising options and then sitting back to let the randomness do its work.

The challenge of building agile organizations is complicated by the fact that these very different concepts are often used interchangeably. For example, armed forces around the world tend to use the term agility as a synonym for "flexibility" and "maneuverability."[31] In business, a recent publication by a leading advisory firm—a thought leader on strategy and management—described agility simultaneously as dynamism, flexibility, speed, nimbleness, responsiveness as well as the organizational ability to renew itself.[32]

To put a fine point on how each of these organizational qualities falls short of agility, consider the case study of IMAX. The company's responses to potentially existential environmental changes were anchored in a compelling strategic vision—to become a key player in the mainstream entertainment industry. This vision guided top-down strategic actions (e.g., decisive entry into the digital space, business model transformations and international expansion) as well as countless bottom-up innovations (e.g., the invention of digital remastering). Instead of defensively reacting to market changes and the actions of other players, IMAX continued to steadfastly pursue its objectives. Concerted efforts were devoted to maintaining resilience in the face of adversity with the intent to resume the offensive posture as soon as possible. Shared understanding of the environment, strategic direction and operating philosophy resulted in keen situational awareness, calculated risk-taking and the unity of effort. In short, IMAX exhibited adaptability, resilience, flexibility, dynamism and antifragility combined. And yet none of these concepts—individually or together—can fully describe IMAX's process, capabilities or the organizational setting that created agility.

Agility is an overarching quality that *encompasses* these other more specialized traits and competences but goes much further. Its distinctive nature, illustrated in the figure below, enables organizations to effectively deal with both threats and opportunities, maintain a bias for offense in both favorable and adverse circumstances, and dominate change through actions that are purposeful, decisive and grounded in the will to win.

Agility: An Overarching Quality

~

In the next three chapters, we'll turn our attention to risk intelligence and its critical role in fostering agility. We'll demonstrate how the fight for risk intelligence and risk radars can empower the detection and assessment of environmental signals, and how strategic calculus can help sift through alternative responses to change. We'll explain how performance and long-term viability can be enhanced by recognizing organizations as dynamic portfolios of risks and by proactively managing them as such. We start by describing the evolution from risk management to risk intelligence, subsequently showing how military thinking can greatly enhance our understanding of risk and uncertainty.

CHAPTER 4

RISK INTELLIGENCE

Some time ago, senior executives of one of the world's largest global conglomerates asked us to review the risk management package used by the firm's board of directors. It was impressive, indeed. All relevant risk types were captured. Thousands of individual risk factors were meaningfully aggregated. Relevant what-if scenarios and histories were clearly presented and creatively visualized. There was just one caveat: while the board felt it had a good handle on the firm-wide picture of risk—and was confident that the company was safe and sound—none of this information was used in shaping strategy and making organizational and business decisions.

This example is reflective of a broader phenomenon. Even at some of the most sophisticated firms, a gap between strategic decision-making and risk management persists. At most companies, according to a recent analysis by McKinsey & Company, the link between business processes and risk management is downright weak. Many organizations can't actually identify or properly measure the full set of their risk exposures. More often than not, backward-looking quantification of risk is done only at a high level and mostly for the purposes of prioritization. Strategic plans, based on incomplete assumptions and risk assessments, tend to focus on a single baseline scenario.[33] Such obvious deficiencies make executives even more reluctant to use risk analyses in shaping critical business and organizational decisions.

To become practically useful to senior leaders, risk management must be transformed into a strategic resource and a key contributor to an organization's performance and relevance. Given the wealth of risk management frameworks, financial models, analytical tools and practical experience accumulated over the last three decades, this can be done. When Leo proposed a new definition of risk intelligence in 2013, his aim was to convey that risk management can indeed become as invaluable in supporting strategy development and execution as business intelligence and competitive intelligence.[34]

Business intelligence helps companies create a holistic view of their businesses and enhance decision-making by analyzing data about their customers, products, operations and drivers of performance.[35] Extending far beyond reporting and visualization tools, business intelligence systems now drive predictive analyses of marketing strategies, improve resource allocation and enhance operational processes. For example, some pharmaceutical companies use sophisticated statistical models to identify health care professionals who offer the greatest sales potential. This information is integrated with statistical analyses that evaluate cost-effectiveness of various promotion channels, helping identify promising customers while minimizing the risks of targeting the wrong ones.

As for competitive intelligence, its systematic collection and analysis of information helps companies better understand their competitive positioning and operating landscapes, including the strengths, weaknesses and plans of rivals. The insights obtained are commonly parlayed into strategy, M&A, R&D, and a wide array of marketing and branding initiatives. One of our corporate clients significantly improved its footprint in a certain B2B market after conducting extensive intelligence analysis that showed that the company's problems in the area stemmed from an overly conservative tolerance for risk. Importantly, this was not apparent by evaluating the firm's risk tolerance on a stand-alone basis, but only in comparison to its main competitors. By deliberately and selectively increasing risk—adding new types of customers, investing in R&D and using balance sheet to capture market opportunities—the company improved its growth rates and equity valuation.

In contrast to the extensive use of these corporate competencies in formulating strategy and improving operations, risk detection and assessment have been seen primarily as defensive and policing functions, reflecting our deep-seated aversion to risk. As the field of risk management evolved, the avoidance and mitigation of threats have become its primary goals. Importantly, it has also turned into an *after the fact* activity: performing safety-and-soundness verifications after strategic, business and investment decisions have already been made.

Business and competitive intelligence didn't emerge as defensive tools used to preserve competitiveness, avoid strategic landmines or remediate operational inefficiencies. They were developed to be useful in proactive, forward-looking decision-making. Risk management can be repositioned to become the same, and its power can be harnessed in ways that are strategic and offense-oriented. To reflect these mandates, Leo defined risk intelligence as:[36]

> *The organizational ability to think holistically about risk and uncertainty, speak a common language and effectively use forward-looking risk concepts and tools in making better decisions, alleviating threats, capitalizing on opportunities and creating lasting value.*

As we discovered while working on this book, this definition closely aligns with the military thinking that sees risk as a fundamental feature of any mission and an invaluable resource for gaining competitive advantage.

Contributions of Military Thinking

One of the most fascinating aspects of developing our understanding of agility has been melding the ways in which risk and uncertainty are understood and exploited across business, finance and the US military. It made us realize how valuable military thinking can be to risk intelligence and agility, both when it comes to high-stakes decision-making and in general.

The military mindset keeps us alert to the fact that our organizations operate in an environment shrouded in fog and friction. This necessitates a relentless fight for risk intelligence, an evaluation of the information it produces, and a careful delineation between risk and uncertainty. This mindset has strategic implications as well. In the US military, strategy is practiced as a calculus of ends, ways, means, *risks* and priorities, with risk being a key driver of decision-making, not an afterthought.

Because most organizations operate in highly competitive environments, adopting a military mindset helps us place adversaries at the center of our decision-making. It becomes integral to our success to constantly evaluate their objectives, risk exposures and access to information. Just like us, our competitors have hidden vulnerabilities. They make judgments based on incomplete or erroneous information. They worry about their capacity to withstand shocks. All of this can be leveraged to our advantage. We have more ways to affect our and others' portfolios of risks than we often realize.[37]

Military thinking helps us stay on the offense, which is reflected in our description of agility as a capacity grounded in the will to win. When we seize the initiative and put our adversaries on the defensive, their ability to exploit our weaknesses is diminished. When we grab an opportunity or develop new capabilities, this often creates a vulnerability for our adversaries. On the flip side, when we are mired in inaction, we often expose ourselves to new threats and yield the initiative to others.

The view that senior leaders are the accountable owners of risk is deeply ingrained in the US military culture, which we argue should be true for all organizations. Military leaders up and down the command chain fully understand that it is an essential responsibility of theirs to understand how risk was assessed and used in shaping action plans. They are required to sharply question whether all relevant threats and ramifications have been considered. They need to be skilled at making high-stake decisions even when information is ambiguous and incomplete. Ultimately, it is the role of senior leaders to determine an acceptable amount of risk that should be taken in the pursuit of objectives.

Transitioning from risk management to risk intelligence involves a profound change in how companies think, monitor their environments, shape and evaluate alternatives, organize themselves, and even how they communicate with stakeholders. Traditional risk management is not abandoned; it plays a vital role in promoting internal and regulatory compliance and fostering safety and soundness. But by instilling an appreciation of the vital role of risk intelligence in all organizational decisions, senior leaders can create a risk-centric mindset and make risk detection and assessment integral to developing situational awareness; achieving growth and profitability targets; and maintaining relevance and a strong brand.

From Risk Management to Risk Intelligence

As we'll explore more fully in the following chapters, turning risk intelligence into a key contributor to the organization's most important decisions is not a matter of generic "best practices." It is a concerted and highly customized process that goes to the heart of the organization's strategy, business model and command-and-control philosophy. It influences measures of success and the design of analytical systems. It has a profound impact on the organizational mindset, culture and decision-making up and down the command chain. When risk intelligence is embraced by the entire organization in this fashion, it becomes integral to the entire Agility Process of detecting, assessing and responding to environmental changes. That's why we consider risk intelligence a pillar of agility.

The Risk Equation

Of course, most organizations know quite well that taking too much risk is an effective way to get into trouble. Yet examples of excessive risk-taking abound. British Petroleum's oil spill and the Space Shuttle Challenger disaster were manifestations of massive operational risk resulting from failures to adopt and comply with basic safety standards. The demise of AIG and Lehman Brothers stemmed from balance sheets exposed to excessive financial risk. The US Army's notable failures to modernize—think of Comanche helicopters, Crusader artillery and the Future Combat System—stemmed from faulty risk management of a broken acquisition process mired in bureaucracy and a lack of accountability.[38]

Since gradual extinctions are far less spectacular, their underlying failures of risk management garner less press. But they can be just as lethal as excessive risk-taking. As the likes of Kodak, Sears and Yahoo demonstrate, risk aversion often leads to stagnation, which stifles strategy and growth-driving ideas. Organizations pass on promising opportunities. Just think of Hewlett-Packard's failure to acquire PWC's consulting arm, which in turn catalyzed IBM's foray into IT advisory services.[39] Lower tolerance for unsuccessful products results in shrinking R&D budgets and lackluster innovation. Overly conservative balance sheets lead to mediocre financial performance. Lower earnings reduce the capacity to retain the best people and absorb economic shocks. A loss of competitiveness, relevance and investor confidence follows, putting pressure on boards and executives to either reassess the risk tolerance or put the company up for sale.

Risk intelligence requires a holistic picture of risk for the entire organization, which necessitates an approach to consistently thinking about risks of different nature and impact. Every organization has a diverse set of risks to be monitored. In the national security realm, risks include not only a potential loss of life and physical assets, but also reputation, credibility, influence and ultimately the loss of a country's independence. In economics, lax monetary policies increase the risks of inflation and financial crises, while hostile regulatory policies threaten economic dynamism and long-term prosperity. In business, companies and investors are exposed to thousands of individual strategic, operational, cybersecurity, reputational and financial risk factors.

The process of constructing a holistic picture starts with defining risk, which is usually done in either absolute or relative terms. Sometimes it's appropriate to think about risk as a possibility of specific harm or loss, such as the potential economic toll of a natural disaster. In other cases, we should use relative terms, such as by defining risk as a possibility that we will not achieve our stated objectives.[40] For example, employee contributions to defined-benefit pension plans are determined by two main factors: promised future payments to retirees and assumptions about future returns on invested assets. If, due to market and credit risks, expected investment returns fail to materialize, the pension plan will have to make up for a shortfall between expectations and reality by reducing future retirement payments, increasing current employee contributions or taking on more risk.

In our framework for agility, we present both absolute and relative risks in terms of their three dynamic and interconnected drivers: *vulnerability, likelihood* and *consequences*:

$$\text{Risk} = \text{Vulnerability} \times \text{Likelihood} \times \text{Consequences}$$

Vulnerability encompasses all sources of exposure to harm or loss, both direct and indirect. Exposure to a cyberattack or a failure of a new product are direct vulnerabilities. In contrast, as we discussed in the previous chapter, our clients' or partners' cybersecurity gaps can become our indirect vulnerabilities. An organization's indirect vulnerabilities may also stem from its internal deficiencies, such as a lack of risk awareness or reliance on the predictions of the future.

Likelihood represents the chance that this harm or loss may indeed materialize.

Consequences describe a multitude of outcomes and side effects of risk, which can be both positive and negative, and both direct and indirect. For example, suppose a reputable bank incurs heavy trading losses due to faulty risk management, governance and incentives (think of JP Morgan's so-called London Whale fiasco in 2012),[41] or a manufacturing firm well known for operational excellence and social responsibility causes a major environmental disaster. In both cases, repercussions will extend far beyond direct consequences (financial losses). Brands will suffer reputational damage, regulatory penalties will be imposed, retention of customers and employees will become challenging. In more extreme cases, access to capital markets may be denied, setting in motion vicious cycles that often lead to ruin.

We propose our risk equation as a heuristic, designed simply to illustrate the main drivers of risk, highlight their interdependence and establish a common language—rather than a literal equation to be used. It's worth noting, however, that risk is in fact often calculated much in this fashion. For example, credit risk is often quantitatively measured as the product of the total loan amount (vulnerability), the likelihood of default and the percentage of the loan amount we won't be able to recoup (consequence).

Another important point about the risk equation is that it should be seen as providing a continuum of possibilities to consider rather than a single scenario. It describes a variety of outcomes, each stemming from the same set of vulnerabilities, each with its own likelihood and consequences. A military campaign may result in a partial advance or retreat, as opposed to an absolute victory or defeat. A launch of a new product has multiple possibilities of being embraced or rejected by consumers. Our stock market investment may generate a moderate monthly gain or loss with minimal consequences, which is very likely. However, our investment may also lose the majority of its value in one month, which is unlikely but extremely consequential. The entire set of possible outcomes and their likelihoods form a probability distribution.

The dynamic relationship between the three drivers of risk must be understood and proactively exploited, and the military mindset is invaluable in this regard. If we are overly concerned about some of our vulnerabilities, this may make us too defensive and reluctant to grab opportunities, diminishing the potential upside. While our vulnerabilities certainly may encourage their aggressive exploitation by adversaries, we may be able to reduce the likelihood of hostile actions by creating heavy penalties for aggression. The ability to uncover the risk equations of our rivals is a mission-critical aspect of fighting for risk intelligence.

The ability to proactively and deliberately alter not only our own risk equations but those of our adversaries is a hallmark of agility. The US military routinely uses deterrence to alter the risk equations of geopolitical adversaries. For example, as the Cold War clearly demonstrated, the likelihood of a nuclear attack by a nation state can be significantly reduced through a threat of mutual destruction. But deterrence is likely to be much less effective in dealing with non-state actors who may gain access to weapons of mass destruction because they organize as diffuse, fluid groups that can't be targeted in the way the nation-states can. It is critical to remember that the effectiveness of deterrence strategies depends on everyone's stakes in the negative consequences.

The prominent and explicit role of adversaries in military thinking has an important implication. In business and finance, risk management often assumes that likelihoods of events are largely beyond our control. A military mindset forces us to question this assumption, given that our actions and capabilities can impact the behaviors of our adversaries, our counterparties and other players within our complex adaptive ecosystem.

Assessing Risk and Opportunity Together

We all have observed a paradoxical duality in the discussion of risk. On the one hand, risk is habitually viewed as a negative, because it stems from vulnerabilities and can result in adverse consequences, including ruin. The role that chance plays in the manifestations of potential outcomes engenders fear that we are not fully in control of our destiny. This is unfortunately true. On the other hand, we all have come to accept that virtually nothing worthwhile can be achieved without well-calculated risk-taking.

Throughout history, many great leaders, writers and philosophers have commented on this dual nature of risk and its centrality in both achieving greatness and suffering demise. Interestingly, one of the most astute observations on this topic came from Earl Nightingale, an acclaimed American speaker, author and US Marine, who miraculously survived the bombing of USS Arizona during the attack on Pearl Harbor. Having devoted a great deal of thinking to human character development and motivation, Nightingale famously suggested that risk and opportunity not only "go together" but should be *measured with the same yardstick*. While, to our knowledge, he never elaborated on what he meant by that, we're struck by how well it describes what the risk equation allows us to do—assess both the upside and the downside of the same risk with one essential mechanism.[42] It helps us see that risk and opportunity are two sides of the same coin.

This does not, of course, mean that both sides are of the same potential value or danger. In fact, as Nassim Nicholas Taleb emphasizes in *Antifragile*, potential losses and opportunities of many human endeavors are asymmetric. He notes, for example, that most lending activities have a very limited upside: if everything goes according to the plan, we will get our money back plus a series of modest interest payments. Meanwhile, the potential downside is incomparably greater: we may lose our entire investment. Investments in R&D have the opposite risk/opportunity profile. If our total R&D budget is determined appropriately, the company's well-being will not be endangered even if most of R&D initiatives fail. On the flip side, as we illustrate throughout the book, R&D can produce innovations that can be transformational, not only in maximizing the chance of survival but in fueling growth, financial performance and relevance. Understanding and actively managing inherent asymmetries between risks and opportunities is another crucial component of risk intelligence.

The agility mindset does not view risk as either inherently positive or negative. Instead, as alluded to earlier, it considers risks indispensable arrows in the quivers of decision makers. If we detect and assess environmental changes adroitly, these arrows enable us to both dynamically manage our portfolios of risks and alter our adversaries' risk equations. This must be done continually and with the same intense focus that senior leaders devote to business initiatives, organizational transformations and strategic investments.

Risk vs. Uncertainty

Another important benefit of the risk equation approach is its applicability not only to risk but also to uncertainty, the concept formally introduced by the great economic theorist Frank Knight nearly a century ago. As Nobel Prize winning economist Edmund Phelps writes in the foreword to Leo's *Financial Darwinism*:

> Knight, observing American business experience, took the unpreceded position that most business decisions, especially strategic ones, are to varying degree steps into the unknown…Each of the possible outcomes of a business venture can be considered to have some probability of occurring, but these probabilities are not known…Knightian uncertainty does not stem from some failure to study on the part of decision makers. Rather, it results from the unknowability of the conditions, future and present, on which the consequences of decisions depend.

Clearly, Knight's assessment of the inherent nature of business environments was closely aligned with Clausewitz's view of all military conflicts being enveloped in fog and friction.

To be agile, organizations must explicitly account for the different nature of risk and uncertainty and develop separate approaches for dealing with the threats and opportunities they present. Uncertainty is fundamentally different from risk because it entails situations where the range of possible outcomes and their likelihoods are not known. For instance, the ecological consequences of using gene editing to eliminate malaria-carrying mosquitos—as well as the likelihood of success—are unknowable. Same applies to attempts to estimate the likelihood of superintelligence taking over the world by 2050 or the dangers that quantum computers may pose to economies and financial markets.[43]

In contrast, risk refers to situations where the range of potential outcomes of an event or an undertaking is known with a reasonable degree of accuracy. Each outcome has some probability of occurring, and these probabilities can be computed using theoretical or empirical models. For instance, we can determine a reasonable range of potential gains and losses that may result from an investment in the Dow Jones Industrial Average index over, say, one year. We can then use statistical analyses of historical information and forward-looking assumptions to estimate the likelihoods of various outcomes. This will provide us with the probability distribution that describes our risks as well as opportunities. In a different example, individual life and car insurance policies can be effectively priced by analyzing historical mortality and accident rates stratified by a variety of relevant factors. Meanwhile, the odds of wins and losses in different forms of casino gambling can be computed using theoretical models.

Importantly, though, thanks to the fog and friction of our competitive environments, even dealing with well-understood risks in practice entails complex decision-making under uncertainty. In fact, depending on the historical or hypothetical environments and assumptions used in analytical models, we may arrive at multiple estimates of risk, some of which may be different by orders of magnitude.[44]

The inherent nature of uncertainty must be acknowledged and explicitly addressed without resorting to prediction or committing to rigid strategies. As we'll demonstrate in Chapter 6, this starts with identifying the areas of uncertainty that may significantly affect our organizations, for instance, technological advances, effects of climate change or changes in geopolitical environments. We can then envision a wide range of possible future scenarios and assess our attendant vulnerabilities and consequences (but not likelihoods!). This will enable us to think through a range of potential actions should various developments, threats and opportunities emerge. Of course, the future will end up being different from our scenarios, and the actions we'll end up taking will undoubtedly be different from pre-existing contingency plans. However, it is this *act of planning* that will foster agility—by improving our understanding of the environment and helping us recognize change, shape risk-intelligent responses and decisively execute when the time is right.

It is the responsibility of senior leaders to delineate risk and uncertainty; understand how various estimates have been derived and scenarios developed; and know what assumptions have been used. This knowledge allows them to make a pivotal act of judgment about the appropriate amount of risk required via a process we refer to as *strategic calculus*.

Strategic Calculus

The three dynamic factors—goals, risk, and capacity—combine in the strategic calculus process, which we heuristically depict as:

$$\text{Goals} \longleftrightarrow \text{Risk} \times \text{Capacity}$$

Capacity is what enables us to take risk in pursuit of stated objectives; it is a description of our resources in the broadest sense. In finance, capacity is usually defined as capital: the monetary resources available to absorb financial losses. In space exploration, capacity may be defined as the ability to sustain human and equipment losses. In business, operational capacity to successfully execute includes human capital, organizational bandwidth and staying power. The risk equation approach significantly broadens our understanding of organizational capacity, presenting it as the mirror image of consequences. As a result, we start considering both direct and indirect consequences of risk. In business, this would entail explicitly evaluating the strategic, regulatory and reputational side effects of financial losses or failures to execute.

The military mindset broadens the concept of capacity even further, making us realize that the intangible human factors—such as the will to win and the physical and moral capacity to prevail—are equally, if not more, important. As Napoleon famously observed, "The moral is to the physical as three is to one." When we overestimate our overall capacity, tangible and intangible, in relation to risk, we endanger our performance and even survival.

In the case of the Space Shuttle Columbia disaster discussed earlier, NASA's senior leadership did a poor job of strategic calculus. When Columbia's wing was damaged during the launch, a new vulnerability emerged, but the risk was deemed acceptable. In essence, NASA misjudged the severity of the damage and the likelihood of a catastrophic failure. The disaster that ensued brought back memories of an equally traumatic event: the 1986 loss of Space Shuttle Challenger that resulted from an even more egregious failure of risk management. Importantly, while assessing the safety of the shuttles and their crews in both cases, decision makers failed to recognize the presence of an entirely different risk equation—that of the United States. In addition to the tragic loss of life, the shuttle disasters damaged societal morale and NASA's reputation to such an extent that the US government became unwilling to bear the risk of additional losses. This affected the US space exploration program for decades to come.

Said differently, in pursuit of its space exploration goals, the US government took the risk of the potential loss of life and assets. The loss of the two shuttles exceeded the country's risk-bearing capacity. The subsequent reduction in risk tolerance prevented the achievement of the original goals.

Cognitive Pitfalls

Throughout the book, we will periodically return to the discussion of how behavioral biases can impair organizational agility. In the previous chapter, we discussed this in relation to the detection and assessment of environmental changes. Not surprisingly, these biases, well known to behavioral economists, can also have a profound impact on risk assessment and strategic calculus. Of special relevance here is our tendency to either ignore or significantly overestimate the likelihood of very rare events, privilege attention to risks we believe can be managed, and assign greater importance to recent history, giving short shrift to events from the distant past that may be relevant to our present risks. The list goes on and on, necessitating an organizational setting where we help each other recognize and preempt the destructive impact of cognitive biases.

The effectiveness of risk assessment and strategic calculus can also be seriously jeopardized by our tolerance or lack of awareness of strategic contradictions. The latter are exemplified by the Joint Comprehensive Plan of Action (2015–16) that is commonly known as the Iran nuclear deal. Western democracies have had a number of vital national interests and security goals related to the Islamic Republic of Iran. They include the imperatives to prevent the country from developing nuclear weapons and to severely limit its willingness and capacity to conduct hybrid warfare against the West. While attempting to address the nuclear non-proliferation objective, the deal alleviated the economic sanctions that were crippling Iran's economy. This provided Iran with resources—without any disincentives—to continue the aggression. In fact, the country's sponsorship of terrorism and engagement in proxy and cyberwarfare have since continued.

Strategic contradictions pose significant risks that must be fully recognized. If in the end, we choose to accept a strategic contradiction, this must be a deliberate and explicit risk-taking decision within our strategic calculus. When implicit strategic contradictions stack on top of each other, the whole strategy can collapse under its own weight of accumulated risk—even if each action could be reasonably explained.

The Fukushima Nuclear Disaster

In the late 1960s, in close coordination with the government of Japan, the Tokyo Electric Power Company (TEPCO) set out to build the Fukushima

Daiichi Nuclear Power Plant. The goals of the initiative reflected Japan's energy needs, the country's commitment to renewable energy and TEPCO's desire to create value for its shareholders. On March 11, 2011, a tsunami caused by an earthquake broke the plant's protective seawall leading to a nuclear accident, a significant release of radioactive materials and total damages in excess of 150 billion dollars.

The Fukushima Daiichi nuclear disaster was a result of both a flawed risk assessment and a flawed strategic calculus by TEPCO, government officials and regulators. First, the risk of a natural disaster that would threaten the plant's viability was significantly underestimated. As Richard Clarke and R. P. Eddy describe in *Warnings*, despite multiple warnings by experts, dozens of safety meetings focused on earthquakes, with the risk posed by tsunamis deemed negligible. In an illustration of the human bias to assign greater weight to recent history mentioned earlier, a moderate tsunami of 1938 was used to justify the risk assessment, while an extremely severe tsunami that happened many centuries earlier was disregarded as an irrelevant "myth." Organizational factors—such as suppression of dissent and willful ignorance—exacerbated the problems. Based on this faulty assessment of risk, which conveniently allowed a reduction of the construction costs, TEPCO lowered the plant's elevation, built a relatively low seawall and placed the backup generators in locations vulnerable to flooding. This increased the plant's vulnerability and reduced its ability to withstand a major natural disaster. As a result, goals, risks and capacity became significantly misaligned.

What was not understood at the time is that the Fukushima risk equation applied not only to the nuclear power plant itself but also to Japan at large, as the flawed strategic calculus during the plant design and construction created new vulnerabilities for the country's energy and economic policies. Japan's capacity to withstand a nuclear power plant meltdown was either overestimated or not considered at all. As a result, at the time of this book's writing, only a fraction of Japanese power plants are operational, and the country's dependence on foreign and non-renewable energy has risen significantly.[45]

The Fukushima nuclear disaster is an illustration of an anti-agile behavior commonly referred to in the financial industry as *borrowing from the future*. While the costs of protection, prevention or deterrence are immediate and tangible, sometimes we cannot help but think that future losses may or may not materialize. In terms of strategic calculus, this happens when we underestimate the likelihoods of adverse events, overestimate our capacity to withstand their negative consequences, or both. As Richard Clarke and R. P. Eddy further explain, TEPCO could have spent more upfront on protective measures: elevate the plant; increase the height of the seawall; and waterproof or relocate the backup generators. Instead it chose to save money by taking none of those precautions and hope for the best. The Japanese government currently views the Fukushima nuclear disaster as *man-made*.[46]

~

When we speak about calculated risk-taking, risk-intelligent decisions and a bias for deliberate action throughout the book, we refer to the organizational ability to understand its risk equations and perform a rigorous strategic calculus. Having just described how we can analyze risk and align it with our goals and resources, in the next two chapters we will turn our attention to the fact that in reality, our organizations are exposed to many interconnected individual risks. We will demonstrate that ways in which these portfolios of risks are conceptualized and managed has a profound impact on the organization's survival and performance—and discuss what all of this means for agility. We start by describing how risk intelligence provides an entirely new perspective for understanding and transforming business models—by viewing organizations as dynamic portfolios of risks.

CHAPTER 5

WHAT BUSINESS ARE WE IN?

In the summer of 2007, several months before the collapse of Bear Stearns, CEO Jimmy Cayne gathered the firm's senior partners for a pep talk. Two of Bear Stearns' flagship mortgage hedge funds just blew up, making Leo and his colleagues deeply concerned. First, there was a distinct possibility that the damage to the firm's brand would be lethal—because Bear Stearns has failed in the area of its greatest perceived competence: mortgage securities and risk management. Moreover, given that the demise of the hedge funds may have been a prelude to a broader crisis, significant worries about Bear Stearns' balance sheet exposures to mortgages and illiquid structured products were more than justified.

Cayne did not seem alarmed. In fact, he predicted that not only would Bear Stearns overcome this "minor" setback, but it would capitalize on all the opportunities that market dislocations invariably present. He went on to elaborate on this promising outlook by stating that the firm has been in business since 1923, through good times and bad, and always came out on top because it was "in a moving business, not in a storage business." By that, of course, Cayne meant that Bear Stearns was in the business of facilitating client transactions and originating complex financial products for sale—as opposed to holding risky assets on the balance sheet and putting the firm's own capital at risk.

Some of the attendees looked visibly bewildered, perhaps having a flashback to the famous scene in the movie *Trading Places,* in which characters discuss the privileges of being a financial broker. It's an enviable position indeed, because no matter whether a client makes or loses money, the broker gets the commission. The problem, of course, was that the view Cayne was expressing was entirely inconsistent with reality. By 2007, Bear Stearns had loaded its balance sheet with illiquid structured products and derivatives, as so many of its investment and commercial banking peers had. These holdings were bound to experience dramatic price declines should the housing market collapse. If, akin to a bank run, the financial losses were to be accompanied by an inability to borrow funds in the capital markets, the threat to the firm could be existential. Bear Stearns had in fact been in the "storage business" for a long time, but that was not reflected either in the beliefs and priorities of its senior executives or in the ways the firm managed risk.[47]

Organizations as Portfolios of Risks

Of course, Cayne was in good company, as a similar misunderstanding of risk was prevalent across the financial industry. Many executive teams and boards we worked with at the time could not connect the dots across a multitude of organizational exposures, which made the evaluation of potential threats, creation of contingency plans and decisive action in the crisis nearly impossible. Importantly, a similar blindness to risk was shared by the external stakeholders. In fact, while the fate of the largest US investment banks could not have been more different,[48] their credit ratings, borrowing costs and price to earnings ratios right before the crisis were virtually identical. In other words, the myriad of investors, counterparties, regulators and rating agencies who analyze companies for a living couldn't distinguish the differences in the financial health and crisis preparedness of firms that ranged from secure to destined for extinction. How can this be?

The paradigm commonly used by external observers to understand companies and business models seems rigorous and comprehensive. We review a company's products, services and organizational structures. We analyze its balance sheet, income statements and drivers of revenues. We discuss its competitive positioning and market presence. We also evaluate external metrics, such as credit ratings, stock prices, borrowing costs and brand equity valuations. Internally, boards and leadership teams use the same set of frameworks, languages and tools in shaping strategy and directing execution.

And yet, despite all this sophistication, corporate earnings and valuations often peak right before major problems. Business extinctions and near-death experiences come as a complete surprise to internal and external stakeholders alike. Critical initiatives fail due to factors that were, in hindsight, within the company's control. To us, this has long implied that something fundamental is not revealed by the conventional approaches. This X-factor is the nature of the organization's portfolio of risks.[49]

This portfolio of risks is an outcome of complex and opaque processes. As a myriad of decisions, actions and transactions continually take place up and down the command chain, various risks get added, eliminated and intertwined. Strategic initiatives, innovations and routine activities—coupled with environmental changes—lead to a continual evolution of this portfolio. The types and magnitudes of individual risks we are exposed to change over time, as does the total amount of risk they entail collectively. Agile organizations relentlessly reassess and actively rebalance their portfolios of risks.

The dangers of not doing so were vividly demonstrated during the European sovereign debt crisis that started in 2009. The board of directors of a well-known multinational company asked us to analyze the firm's near-death experience. Our task was to uncover the key drivers of huge financial losses that were not readily apparent. They could have been caused by an inviable business model, faulty risk management or governance, cultural deficiencies or a variety of other factors. We were to offer recommendations on how to build a more resilient and risk-intelligent organization.[50]

From the outset, the language used by directors and senior executives in describing pivotal strategic decisions was noteworthy. Following the Internet bubble-burst of 2001 and 2002, they explained, the company acquired assets from distressed competitors at bargain prices. Subsequently, the firm embarked on several successful firm-wide product innovation initiatives, significantly increasing market share and paving the way to higher earnings. Vertical integration of select business lines followed a few years later, leading to economies of scale and greater profitability. The decade was capped off by transformational acquisitions that extended the company's reach to new market segments. All of these actions were well-received by Wall Street analysts, credit rating agencies and shareholders, leading to impressive stock price performance.

There was just one problem. This narrative provided absolutely no warning for what was to follow: financial losses, depletion of capital, paralysis of the management team and denied access to capital markets. The analysis of the company's strategic actions from the perspective of risk helped zero in on the key factor: behind "transformational" M&A transactions, "innovative" product development and "bold" restructurings lurked ever-greater risk-taking. Purchases of "bargain-priced" assets resulted in greater credit risk on the asset side of the balance sheet. Product innovation embedded significant market risk in the company's liabilities. Vertical integration introduced an entirely new set of foreign exchange and operational risks that the company was not equipped to manage. Acquisitions of competitors with highly leveraged balance sheets stretched the firm's capacity to absorb market shocks.

The true impact of this process on safety and soundness was largely invisible to external stakeholders. It was also misunderstood internally, with the company's senior leaders misjudging risk in a number of ways. Chief among them was a failure to recognize that strategic initiatives mentioned earlier largely entailed systematic risks.

All risks can be divided into two fundamentally different categories: idiosyncratic and systematic. Idiosyncratic risks apply to individual organizations, assets or initiatives and, therefore, can be managed through diversification. In contrast, systematic risks represent changes in financial markets, economies and political environments. In business and finance, systematic risks—which include interest rates, stock indices, economy-wide credit defaults and currency exchange rates—are driven by economic cycles, monetary and fiscal policies, and supply and demand. Unlike idiosyncratic risks, systematic risks can't be managed through diversification. Changing our exposures to them requires financial transactions, such as restructuring of assets and liabilities, derivatives hedging or insurance.

The company's leaders assumed that the overall risk being taken on would be diversified across these seemingly different corporate actions, which was incorrect. This assumption could not be tested because the company didn't have the capacity to aggregate disparate exposures. Also, in estimating risk, the company relied on the data from a very tranquil market environment, which created a false sense of comfort and led to excessive risk-taking. All of this resulted in a faulty strategic calculus, with goals, risks and risk-bearing capacity ending up dramatically misaligned.

Misunderstanding and mismanagement of the portfolio of risks—not the company's strategy, lack of competitiveness or ineffective execution—largely determined the outcome. The company did not invest in creating a comprehensive firm-wide picture of risk, which prevented it from identifying and monitoring environmental conditions that could send it into a tailspin. Contingency plans involving risk mitigation were absent. While the company was teetering on the edge of demise—unaware, exposed and unprepared—everyone's focus and efforts were elsewhere.

Our client's woes belong to a whole category of anti-agile behaviors that we call *flying blind*. We fly blind when we do not fully understand our portfolio of risks, its role in our business model or its connection to our operating landscape. We may be simply unaware of certain risks faced by our organization. For the risks that have been identified, we may misjudge their nature or risk equations, skewing strategic calculus. Or we may fail to connect our risk exposures to the relevant changes in the environment, as Bear Stearns failed to link its "storage business" with the emerging cracks in the US housing market. Similarly, Blockbuster failed to link its strategic risk to the possibility that streaming would become a dominant entertainment delivery mechanism. Of course, flying blind is antithetical to agility, and so is the dominant organizational practice we discuss next.

How to Spot a Sitting Duck

Over the years, we've encountered many instances where an organization effectively identifies and assesses a risk it is facing but then deems the risk "inherent in its nature of business." Leaders, therefore, decide to leave it unmanaged.[51] In *Financial Darwinism*, Leo demonstrated that such practices—which he called static business models—leave organizations at the mercy of external forces, making them the proverbial sitting ducks.

Player concussions have been long considered the nature of business of the US National Football League. Annual diagnosed incidents averaged about 7.5 per team, which seemed acceptable to the individual teams and the league as a whole.[52] All of this changed as the increasing numbers of retired NFL players developed major cognitive and memory problems, prompting researchers to link repeated head traumas to degenerative brain diseases. As a consequence of this deliberately unmanaged risk, the NFL was hit with multi-billion-dollar class action lawsuits. Today, the league is actively managing the concussion risk using a number of strategies. They include greater funding for medical and neuroscience research, helmet engineering advancements and changes in helmet-hit and other game rules.[53]

In business and finance, static business models almost always involve systematic risks. Since these risks fluctuate with economic cycles and other macroeconomic forces, the financial performance of companies tends to be volatile and cyclical.[54] For example, the operating earnings of multinational companies (who believe that bearing foreign currency risk is the nature of their business) can be wiped out when currency exchange rates move against them. Earnings of advertising companies and mortgage originators usually decline during recessions. Earnings of small banks that do not actively manage macroeconomic credit risks decrease during recessions and increase during expansions. Similarly, asset managers who ride the same risk exposures across economic cycles tend to deliver cyclical and volatile investment returns.

In addition to causing problems of volatile and cyclical performance, static business models are antithetical to agility because they make companies and investors especially vulnerable to the vicious cycles that have been prominently on display over the past thirty years. The financial industry serves as an instructive case study.

Vicious Cycles of Risk-Taking

During long economic expansions, periods of loose monetary policies or market bubbles, compensation for bearing risk declines. When faced with the attendant earnings pressures, agile financial firms and investors carefully assess the environment, evaluate risk equations and use strategic calculus to analyze alternatives. They may decide to reduce earnings targets and tell shareholders to expect lower returns until the market conditions improve. Alternatively, they may decide to deliberately increase risk in order to maintain the same level of earnings, or try to improve profitability, or explore new products and markets that offer more attractive opportunities. The whole process will be explicit: if greater risk-taking ends up being the preferred solution, it will be accompanied by the heightened risk awareness, protective actions and contingency plans.

Almost invariably, financial firms and investors with static business models respond to earnings pressures by increasing risk within existing businesses or taking on unfamiliar, seemingly diversified risks. The extent of this additional risk-taking is often misunderstood, especially in relation to the firm's capacity to withstand losses. In other cases, players may recognize the increased vulnerability but continue, in the words of former Citigroup CEO Chuck Prince, dancing while the music is playing. When such behaviors take hold en masse, a vicious cycle ensues. Greater risk-taking further compresses the market compensation for risk. In turn, to keep up with their peers and earnings targets, players increase leverage and risk, and so on. As we'll explore more fully in Chapter 9, at such times, epidemics of flawed narratives and ideas often add fuel to the fire, providing a false sense of comfort and leading to a collective blindness to risk and uncertainty.

Vicious Cycles of Deleveraging

Having responded to earnings pressures through excessive risk-taking, sitting ducks find themselves at the mercy of forces beyond their control when the music invariably stops playing. Thanks to an unpredictable catalyst or a tipping point, the adaptive environment that has been hovering close to the edge of chaos descends into a financial crisis. As the crisis starts to unfold, initial market dislocations lead to a dramatic increase in risk aversion. In the words of the former Federal Reserve Chairman Alan Greenspan, the "animal spirits" that drive risk-taking and economic activity in normal environments succumb to fears.[55] Amidst fog and friction, inaction and fight-and-flight responses displace well-considered deliberate action. Prices of financial assets—such as stocks, bonds, loans and companies—drop while credit defaults start to increase.

When sitting ducks are forced to deleverage—due of margin calls, inadequate capitalization or decrease in the internal tolerance for risk—they try to sell at-risk assets only to discover an absence of buyers even in usually deeply liquid financial markets.[56] Meanwhile, access to funding and capital dries up even for well-known and stable firms. As a last measure, holdings that have not yet been affected by the crisis are sold, with loss contagion spreading across financial markets. Systematic risks start to move in unison, rendering "diversification" strategies ineffective. Most financial crises have exhibited this pattern since the crash of 1987.

The capacity to deeply understand and actively manage portfolios of risks is a hallmark of agility. Organizations that possess this ability become positioned to mitigate threats and capture opportunities, both in normal environments and during crisis. In contrast, organizations that don't fully grasp or actively manage their portfolios of risks—due to lack of risk intelligence, indecisiveness or deliberate management choices—yield the initiative and find themselves at the mercy of the forces they don't control. In the next chapter, we will discuss the practical approaches to monitoring and managing risk and uncertainty within the Agility Process.

With respect to agility, risk intelligence plays another important role: it equips us with a new way of thinking about organizations, business models and strategic initiatives. We turn to this topic next.

Business Models through the Prism of Risk

In warfare, the most important task facing statesmen or commanders is, according to Clausewitz, to understand "the kind of war on which they are embarking; neither mistaking it for, nor trying to turn it into, something that is alien to its nature." For all organizations, an analogous act of judgment entails answering a seemingly straightforward question: "What business are we in?"

Even for senior leaders, equipped with all available information about their organizations, rigorously answering this question can be challenging. For external stakeholders—such as customers, investors or regulators— the task can be especially daunting. One reason is that organizational narratives—internal and external—often conflate missions, goals, ways and means, confusing "what we do," "how we do it" and "why we do it." These narratives also fail to describe the risks we take in pursuit of our objectives and ways in which we rebalance these risks over time. This critical aspect of "the business we are in" remains hidden.

Take Google's parent company Alphabet, Inc. as an example. Building on Google's original vision of organizing the world's information and making it "universally accessible and useful," Alphabet, Inc. runs a number of complementary businesses. The groundbreaking search engine has been supplemented by software offerings, a cloud computing business and a wide range of digital technology products. The company has made a number of forays into hardware, such as with its Chromebook computer, Home digital assistant and Google Glass. In parallel, the firm is developing driverless cars and space exploration technologies. So, Alphabet can be described as a multifaceted technology platform that spans digital and digitally enhanced products and services, software and hardware.

This familiar narrative obscures the fact that out of approximately $90 billion in revenues in 2016, close to 90 percent came from advertising. In fact, Alphabet's many offerings—which differ significantly in descriptions, activities and underlying technologies—are all aimed at maximizing the time people spend online so that Google can show them more ads. The company's popular sites and apps, and its large online real estate through partner sites, are devised to allow for highly targeted advertising, thereby justifying the fees it charges advertisers. From this perspective, Alphabet is, most fundamentally, a digital advertising firm.[57]

Just like their technology counterparts, digital advertising firms face a number of familiar risks that must be managed. When the upstart competitor Instagram tried to lure away users' eyeballs, Facebook mitigated strategic risk by purchasing the company in 2012. In the years ahead, Google will have to defend its digital ad dominance against Amazon, which is rapidly gaining ground in the area of consumer product searches.[58] Digital advertisers, like all organizations, face cybersecurity threats exemplified by the massive Equifax breach in 2017. They also face the "nature-of-business" financial risks since advertising revenues tend to decline during economic recessions.

In other important respects, portfolios of risks of digital advertising firms are drastically different from those of technology companies. Significant problems arise when this is not recognized by the companies' leaders and external stakeholders, as showcased by the assorted problems that have plagued another de facto digital advertiser, Facebook, since 2016. To be competitive and effective in selling ads, digital advertising firms often house and exploit vast amounts of sensitive consumer data. Safeguarding this information is subject to a number of risks. If data is provided to third parties in violation of consumer privacy laws, financial, reputational and regulatory risks arise. This appears to have been the case when sensitive information and habits of up to 50 million Facebook users were allegedly used by Cambridge Analytica during the Brexit referendum and the 2016 US presidential election.

Digital advertisers expose themselves to reputational risks when they fail to prevent nefarious actors from using their platforms to spread misinformation and sow instability, as with the use of Facebook ads by Russia. When users are manipulated or discriminated—as in the 2019 allegation that Facebook violated the Fair Housing Act by allowing real estate companies to improperly target potential customers—this leads to reputational, financial and regulatory risks, some of which may be existential.[59] Facebook's problems have stemmed from its failure to adequately assess and manage its entire portfolio of risks—and from the failure to recognize new vulnerabilities created by pivotal business decisions.

Entity	Nature of Business (conventional view)	Nature of Business (portfolio of risks)
Bear Stearns	"Moving business"	"Storage business"
Alphabet	Conglomerate whose businesses include a search engine, software, hardware, self-driving cars, and space exploration	Digital advertising firm with a variety of ancillary businesses
General Motors (pre-bailout)	Car manufacturer	Health insurer and pension benefits provider that makes cars and runs a financial institution
The Iraq War (2003-11)	War of liberation and regime change, followed by brief stability operations and withdrawal	Regime change; sectarian civil war created by a power vacuum; prolonged counter-insurgency campaign
Wachovia	Retail and commercial bank focused on deposit growth and client service	Mortgage real estate investment trust funded by short-term liabilities
Freddie Mac (pre-bailout)	Mortgage government-sponsored enterprise that fosters home ownership	Undercapitalized monoline insurance company
MF Global	Brokerage firm	Macro hedge fund
U.S. Government (credit programs)	Public policy that supports vital industries; spurs innovation; stimulates economic growth	Investment management

By carefully evaluating portfolios of risks and deciding how they should be managed and altered over time, we become better equipped to shape strategy, evaluate alternatives and mitigate threats. We also gain new ways to examine and articulate the nature of our business. This often helps uncover discrepancies between the business we think we are in, the business we are actually in and the business we want to be in. The power of this approach can be illuminated by considering some additional cases of well-known organizations and campaigns.

General Motors

Before its bankruptcy in 2009, one of the largest in US history, GM was generally viewed as a traditional car manufacturer, indeed one that may have been too traditional. Its multi-decade loss of the market share—from 50 percent in the 1960s to 20 percent in 2009—has been driven by high costs and inferior quality. During the global financial crisis of 2008–09, the company had to be bailed out by the US government due to $70 billion in losses resulting from typical risks of car manufacturers in tough economic times. As job losses across the country intensified and access to credit dried up, auto sales plummeted. Losses at GM's financing arm, GMAC, made matters considerably worse. GM looked poised for extinction, and with the risk that posed to the auto industry and the greater economy, the Obama administration determined it had no choice but to step in.

This narrative fails to account for the nature and impact of the company's portfolio of risks, including the mismatch between its assets and liabilities. By 2009, GM had ten retirees for every active employee, dangerous exposure to fixed costs and tens of billions in pension liabilities. With hourly compensation already 25 percent higher than that of foreign automakers in the US, benefits added another 20 percent. A typical well-run industrial company focuses on profitable growth while allocating an appropriate share of revenues to employee benefits. At GM, the tail was wagging the dog.

Exorbitant costs of healthcare and pension benefits, and their associated risks, drove business decisions and skewed strategic calculus. The company was unable to proactively mitigate these risks due to economic pressures and rigid labor contracts. All of this ended up impairing the firm's competitiveness and financial viability.

If one examines the company through this lens, pre-bailout GM comes off not so much as a traditional car manufacturer but rather a health insurer and pension benefits provider that tries to fulfill these obligations by making cars and running a risky financial institution.[60]

The 2003-2011 Iraq War

Prior to the invasion of Iraq in 2003, the US government and military leaders devoted significant resources to collecting intelligence on Iraq's weapons of mass destruction and military capabilities. Preparation and planning for the campaign reflected the prevailing view: US armed forces will conduct a swift war of liberation and regime change, a relatively brief period of stabilization operations will follow, weapons of mass destruction will be seized, the reins will be given to an emergent Iraqi government and then the forces will quickly withdraw. As best described by the Strategic Studies Institute, accompanying this view were the following expectations. The US military would be warmly greeted by the Iraqi people as liberators. The country will quickly transition to a democratic political system and a free-market economy. Iraq's police and military will secure the country, while oil revenues will fund reconstruction and economic recovery. Iraq's neighbors will help or at least remain neutral. Stabilizing and rebuilding Iraq will be easier than removing Saddam Hussein from power.[61]

Of course, the above characterization of the "business we were in" was far from reality partly because of the inadequate intelligence gathering, analysis and planning that led to incomplete understanding of the full set of risks that invading the country and removing Saddam Hussein from power entailed. Assessments also inadequately factored in Iraq's societal structures and religious dynamics, such as the Sunni-Shia divide. Critical assumptions about potential breakdowns of political power and the security infrastructure, as well as the American public's risk appetite for leaving Iraq in chaos, were not challenged or war-gamed. And, of course, the reality turned out to be different from expectations thanks to the ever-present friction.

After the invasion, the US became embroiled in refereeing the emergent sectarian civil war created by a power vacuum. A prolonged counter-insurgency (CI) campaign to support the new government by safeguarding elections and helping build governmental capacity followed. As policy and strategy settled down to this longer and more complex CI task, the assessment process used by military forces was adjusted in ways that allowed for more accurate risk management and risk intelligence. Deliberately assessing what activities and conditions needed to be monitored over time and defining what success looked like became a priority across the theater. Trends that indicated what might accelerate success and what potential threats might emerge and derail the campaign were developed, becoming the focus of the fight for risk intelligence. All of this effort was made possible by redesigning and clearly articulating the purpose of the strategy across the command. This process of realizing over time the business the US was really in, and getting back on track, extended through 2011 when Chuck served as the Commanding General of Multinational Corps in Iraq.

The Wachovia Fire Sale

As we alluded to in the Bear Stearns example, many significant risks faced by companies are not visible to external stakeholders, especially when it comes to financial services firms. In general, it is very challenging to understand a company's portfolio of risks and ways in which it is managed based on standard financial disclosures that corporations are required to make. When companies have hidden contingent liabilities or use derivatives and structured products to alter their risk equations, the task becomes virtually impossible. As a result, the true nature of business models is often revealed only when risks manifest themselves in losses and breakdowns, especially during economic and financial crises.

In 2008, Wachovia held over $700 billion in assets and was one of the largest and best performing bank holding companies in the US. The firm consistently ranked as the national leader in organic growth. Among retail banks, it was ranked highest in customer experience. CEO Ken Thomson was adamant about these priorities. He argued that customer service and deposit growth were the optimal revenue strategies for a retail bank. The bank's acquisition of Golden West Financial in 2006 seemed like a smart implementation of that vision. Golden West was the country's second largest savings and loan association at the time, with a 285-branch network concentrated in the Midwest and Western states where Wachovia had little presence. Particularly appealing was Golden West's considerable footprint in the fast-growing market of California.

Yet, in April 2008, Wachovia announced it was cutting 500 jobs and dramatically lowered its dividend. It also went on the hunt for a $7 billion capital infusion. In May, the company's reporting for the first quarter revealed it had lost $707 million, and Ken Thompson was forced out. By July, losses had skyrocketed to $10 billion. Then, on September 26, almost $5 billion in deposits were withdrawn in what was dubbed a silent bank run. The stock plunged 27 percent. To forestall the inevitable collapse, federal regulators rushed in, facilitating a frenzied sale of the company, with Citigroup being first in line, but Wells Fargo ultimately prevailing.[62]

Wachovia failed because its risk exposures linked to the US housing market were not appropriately assessed and managed. Wachovia's holdings of mortgage loans and securities were steadily growing in the build-up to the financial crisis. The bank's exposure to a housing market collapse was supercharged by the acquisition of Golden West whose balance sheet was loaded with risky mortgages. The bank run showcased the bank's vulnerability to customer deposit withdrawals. So, with respect to its portfolio of risks, Wachovia was not a deposit-gathering machine that excelled in client service. It was more akin to a mortgage real estate investment trust that was highly leveraged through short-term liabilities.

Many other companies and investors were hit hard by the financial crisis. In some cases, it was revealed that business models had changed in ways that piled on risk. For example, MF Global, a once sleepy brokerage that was supposed to simply facilitate client transactions, began acting like a hedge fund, and its outsized bets on European government markets ended up bringing it down. In other cases, the crisis showed a lethal misalignment of goals, risks and the capacity to withstand losses. For instance, the government-sponsored enterprise Freddie Mac, which was supposed to be in the business of fostering home ownership as a public policy objective, ended up looking like an undercapitalized monoline insurance company.

There was nothing inevitable about the failures of financial institutions during the crisis. Like some banks and investors who fared well, they could have detected and assessed the cracks in the housing market early on and shaped decisive responses, coming out of the crisis in a position to capture the opportunities it presented. Importantly, these failures were not all the same. Some of them did stem from lacking risk intelligence: key risk exposures were not identified until they started to manifest in losses, risk equations were misjudged, risk-bearing capacity was vastly overestimated thanks to faulty strategic calculus. However, in other failures, all of this was amplified—and sometimes caused—by organizational and leadership deficiencies that we'll explore in the following chapters. They included the suppression of dissent, indecisiveness, overconfident actions grounded in gut feelings and micromanagement that deprived organizations of both situational awareness and execution dexterity.

The US Government as an Asset Manager

When once-promising solar manufacturer Solyndra declared bankruptcy in September 2011, it left the US Federal Government holding the bag for $535 million. The company had been a beneficiary of a guaranteed loan program run by the Department of Energy (DOE) first instituted by the George W. Bush administration and then considerably expanded by President Obama under the American Recovery and Reinvestment Act of 2009, better known as the stimulus package.

A chorus of commentators seized on Solyndra's failure, arguing that the federal government had no business investing in private companies, let alone risky startups. When the FBI raided Solyndra's headquarters and launched a criminal investigation, congressional hearings were held to look into the decision to provide the loan. Presidential candidate Mitt Romney held a campaign event in front of the Solyndra headquarters and called the company "a symbol of gross waste" of public funds stemming from the failure "to understand the basic nature of free enterprise in America."[63]

But the problem with the government investment in Solyndra was not the strategy of bolstering US competitiveness in a vital technology sector using taxpayer money. Instead, the Solyndra losses stemmed from the fact that in order to advance its public policy goals, the Department of Energy had to become a de facto professional investment manager—and it was pretty bad at it. In addition to failing to identify a key strategic risk that ended up bringing the company down,[64] the DOE exhibited significant due diligence deficiencies. According to the 2015 Inspector General report, Solyndra had provided the DOE "statements, assertions and certifications that were inaccurate and misleading," and the DOE did not detect the inaccuracies. Additionally, the DOE failed to request information that was described by the report as "highly relevant" to the risk assessment of the loan, which was deliberately omitted by Solyndra.[65]

This report came on the heels of a 2013 study by the White House Office of Management and Budget (OMB) that uncovered similar shortcomings across federal credit programs that totaled approximately 3.5 *trillion* dollars. The OMB subsequently directed government agencies to identify and adopt best private-sector practices in credit risk management, an effort we were privileged to be a part of.[66] In order to improve public policy outcomes at the lowest cost and risk for taxpayers, credit programs were instructed to set up robust and accountable management and oversight structures, deepen the knowledge of modern risk management and develop systems to support effective, data-driven, real-time evaluation of risk. In recognition of the business federal credit programs are actually in, the overall goal of it all was described as *proactive portfolio management.*

A parallel process spearheaded by the US Department of the Treasury was taking place at the 30,000-foot level. It was prompted by the massive outlays the US government had made during the 2008–09 financial crisis: putting Fannie Mae and Freddie Mac into conservatorship, bailing out financial and auto industries, and providing liquidity to companies and investors. Many of these outlays were manifestations of risk exposures and contingent liabilities that had not been previously recognized. So, the department set out to meticulously catalog and analyze, for the first time in US history, the entire portfolio of risk exposures inherent in federal assets and liabilities under its purview. This indispensable first step has led to big-picture strategic questions reflective of the business the Treasury was in as steward of taxpayers' assets.[67] How should this vast portfolio be aggregated and intuitively presented? What is the appropriate relationship between individual agencies (risk takers) and the Treasury (the owner of risk)? How should this portfolio be managed and governed—both in normal environments and in times of crisis? The process of answering these questions is ongoing.

Critics have argued that the US government has no business being a lender or a venture capitalist and that it should stick to public policy instead. In reality, the two are closely linked. In an environment of rapid change, persistent geopolitical conflict and the arms race of advanced technologies, the nation cannot afford *not to* take risk to secure its future prosperity and security. Vital national interests in cybersecurity, genomic science, artificial intelligence, quantum computing, agricultural innovation, energy, weaponry and so many other fast-evolving areas of technology may need to be advanced by adroitly deploying taxpayer money. In order to achieve that, the US government will need to become a better lender and investor, capable of actively managing portfolios of assets and risks. Only then will it generate the best public policy return on investments—all while safeguarding taxpayer assets.

Corporate Responses to Change

Over the years, as we have worked with a variety of companies, institutional investors and government agencies on unmasking, assessing and managing their portfolios of risks, we have helped them evaluate the nature of their business from this perspective. Throughout, many of them have described this as a process of *illumination* that reveals the reality that had previously been hidden. This work has called to mind Robert Kegan's theory of transformational learning, which deals with how we construct our understanding of reality and how this process changes over time. There is, in fact, a profound difference between learning new information and skills as opposed to making a leap to new, more complex, and more versatile ways of *meaning making*. Representing organizations and business models as evolving portfolios of risks has been, in our experience, such a leap.[68]

This approach is becoming especially important as companies across industries and sectors are responding to technological advances and accelerating disruption by undertaking dramatic business model augmentations and transformations. Many of these strategic actions—implemented through M&A, new products and new services—can and often do change portfolios of risks, necessitating a significant change in the way companies organize, manage and govern themselves. Sometimes, these actions seem like a fundamental change of the organization's very reason for being. Among some of the notable examples:

- Apple is aiming to double the size of its services business by 2021, while simultaneously expanding into production and distribution of original entertainment content.

- John Deere, the world's largest manufacturer of tractors and harvesting combines, is extending its financing business beyond equipment, now providing programs to assist farmers with short-term credit needs and in the process becoming one of the largest agricultural lenders.

- Microsoft is transforming from a model driven by the lynchpin of Windows to one centered on its Azure cloud-computing and Office productivity services businesses.

- PepsiCo is evolving from a model centered on selling sugary drinks and unhealthy snacks into the new terrain of nutritious foods, such as with its acquisition of Bare Snacks.

- With its acquisition of Time Warner, AT&T is expanding beyond the telecom business into entertainment.

- CVS, which is renaming itself into CVS Health Corp, is transitioning from a drugstore chain into a health care provider by purchasing health insurer Aetna.

Meanwhile, auto manufacturers, Google, Uber and others are rapidly developing self-driving car businesses. Office-sharing companies, such as WeWork, and online real estate database companies, such as Zillow, are starting to purchase real estate. Business schools are setting up venture capital funds. As an embodiment of it all, Amazon is expanding into a vast array of new businesses: movie making; physical retail by opening its own branded stores; grocery businesses by building on the acquisition of Whole Foods; and Amazon Key, a service that enables customers to manage deliveries remotely. As a result, describing the nature of its business and its reason for being is increasingly challenging. These moves represent bold, proactive responses to the changing landscape of opportunities and threats. The fog, friction and uncertainty these organizations are contending with are arguably more disorienting than ever before in business history.

The point of rigorous and steadfast assessment of the organization's nature of business—including from the perspective of risk—is certainly not to dissuade movements into new areas of business or new types of risk. Such moves are often vital and a hallmark of agility. With so much innovation unfolding, firms that fail to embrace possibilities, and in some instances make bold changes to their business models, will face the greatest risk of all, that of extinction. When losses occur due to such moves, plenty of critics usually jump in to argue that an organization never should have made the attempt. More appropriate is support for transformational corporate actions, but only when accompanied by a rigorous consideration of how they influence the entire portfolio of risks, and balance it with goals and resources.

~

Successfully navigating disruption and complexity—by managing our existing businesses and entering new ones—will require a continuous reassessment of two moving parts: environmental changes and our portfolio of risks. In the next chapter, we describe a holistic process that enables this and powerful tools that facilitate it, such as risk radars. This paves the way to the discussion of how portfolios of risks should be dynamically managed.

CHAPTER 6

THE RISK LEVERS OF AGILITY

Sectarian violence between Catholics and Protestants in Ireland dates back over eight hundred years, to when English King Henry II invaded the emerald isle in 1171 and, with the Pope's blessing, asserted Catholic authority. The Irish did not take kindly to the aggression. When a later Henry, the Tudor King Henry VIII, controversially left the Church due to his desire to divorce and founded the Church of England, Catholic-held land in Ireland was awarded to supporters of Henry. After his daughter Elizabeth, an ardent anti-Catholic Protestant, took power, she launched a campaign against Catholicism in Ireland and awarded many more Catholic-owned estates to Protestants. Multiple Irish rebellions followed, all bloodily put down. Nonetheless, Catholicism continued to flourish and by 1921–22, when the predominantly Catholic Irish Republican Army and associated nationalist groups forced separation from Britain and the establishment of the Irish Free State—later renamed The Republic of Ireland—the Protestant population had concentrated in the northeast of the country. Northern Ireland was established as a separate entity, and a strong Protestant loyalist majority opted to remain in the United Kingdom. But conflict continued to brew.

Two mutually exclusive visions of national identity and belonging held sway in Northern Ireland. The Catholic minority wanted to join with the

Republic, while the Protestant majority continued to strongly prefer remaining part of Britain. During cultural and political upheavals of the 1960s, the tensions flared ushering in "The Troubles" with escalating hostilities between republican and loyalist paramilitaries, civil rights groups and British security forces. Bombings and sectarian killings terrorized the public with stories of funerals and horrifying images of beatings, shootings and bombed out buildings dominating the news. Violence persisted for three decades claiming over 3,500 lives, and in 1995, when President Bill Clinton appointed former US Senate Majority Leader George Mitchell as a Special Envoy to Northern Ireland, the prospects for peace and reconciliation seemed dim.

In this new role, Mitchell chaired a commission studying the thorny issue of the disarmament of the paramilitary organizations. That had been made a condition of participation in negotiations. But the Sinn Fein party, affiliated with the Irish Republican Army, had refused to give up its weapons as a precondition, and without Sinn Fein involved in negotiations, an agreement would not be tenable. Mitchell found himself deeply engaged in an extraordinarily complex conflict situation, about which he would later say he was "wrapped in a cocoon of naiveté."[69] Yet he made vital contributions to the commission's work, and a set of guidelines it issued for conducting peace talks came to be called The Mitchell Principles. He was subsequently appointed to chair the peace negotiations, which culminated in the Good Friday Agreement of 1998, establishing lasting peace. In thinking about this historic process, our intuition told us that Mitchell's efforts must have entailed a great deal of risk intelligence. Our conversations with him confirmed that.

Senator Mitchell fought doggedly and with great patience and acute observation for the risk intelligence that guided his approach to chairing the commission and then leading the negotiations. He explained to us that developing a detailed understanding of the origins and history of the conflict was a critical priority, both prior to arriving in Ireland and throughout his engagement in the talks. He did extensive research on the topic and spoke to leading experts on both sides of the Atlantic. He also established relationships with key players, closely studying their personalities and motivations, and listening for hours and hours to their views. The commitment he made to understanding the nuances of the perspective of all parties was attested to with Irish flair by one participant, Reg Empey of the Ulster Unionist party, who said "I think anybody who knows anything about the hours he [Mitchell] has had to sit listening to us squabbling and arguing must give him good credit."[70]

Given how intractable the conflict had been, Senator Mitchell searched for any developments in the conflict situation that could offer an opening to novel approaches, suggesting perhaps previously unavailable solutions. He found three such environmental changes. None of them, he noted, was fully apparent to him until the groups had reached certain critical points in the negotiations.

First, he perceived an important evolution that had occurred in the public attitude toward the conflict by the mid- to late-1990s. On all sides, the fear and anxiety about the violence, particularly the targeting of civilians in bombings of pubs, hotels, parks and shops, had led to an overwhelming desire that attacks be stopped.

Second, Mitchell perceived a sense of urgency about reaching an agreement among the representatives of the opposing sides. As discussions proceeded, he noticed that members of all groups of participants increasingly spoke about their fear of continuing violence. In the language of diplomacy, the parties had reached the point of a mutually hurting stalemate—a situation in which all parties to a conflict have determined they cannot prevail by a return to hostilities. All feared renewed violence more than they feared ramifications of agreeing to engage in negotiations. The situation was, as diplomacy scholars say, ripe—opportune for the intervention of a third party to mediate a resolution.

The third environmental change he noted was that women were entering the political process in Northern Ireland to a greater extent. Many of these female politicians had been significantly influenced by their direct personal experience of the conflict and were determined to prevent ongoing tragedies. They brought a new vigor to the government's efforts.

Having made these observations, Mitchell focused on getting the commitment from all parties not to engage in any further violence as the precondition for being admitted into negotiations and advised that the de-commissioning of the paramilitaries' weaponry no longer be a precondition. The issue of decommissioning would be addressed by parallel negotiations.[71] All parties deemed necessary to the negotiations agreed to the terms, a ceasefire began, and talks got underway. The Good Friday Agreement was signed on April 10, 1998, after an intense 36-hour period of non-stop dis-cussions, setting forth a new power-sharing structure for the government of Northern Ireland and clearly defining, at last, the nature of the relationships between Northern Ireland, the Republic of Ireland and the United Kingdom.[72] Mitchell's intelligence about the overwhelming desire of the public for peace was confirmed when in referendums about the Agreement were held in May 1998, over 70 percent of the public in Northern Ireland and nearly 95 per-cent in the Republic of Ireland voted in favor.

The environmental changes that paved the way to the Good Friday Agreement could not be imagined or predicted. They had to be detected, which required, in Clausewitz's words, "a sensitive and discriminating judg-ment" and "a skilled intelligence to scent out the truth."

How can this capacity be cultivated for an organization at large and institutionalized via analytical tools, processes and cultures?

Fighting for Risk Intelligence

Effective detection of change requires keen situational awareness. In order to recognize emerging threats and opportunities, however faint at first, our organi-zations must carefully study how technological, geopolitical and societal trends are affecting today's operating environments and shaping those of tomorrow. We must be sensitive to changes in economic, regulatory and financial market condi-tions; have detailed, real-time information about our evolving portfolio of risks; and understand the relevant competitive factors, including, to the extent possible, the intentions and risk equations of our adversaries.

When we set out to systematically acquire the knowledge and infor-mation required—the process we refer to as *fighting for risk intelligence*—we are faced with two distinct challenges. Ironically, the first stems from the fact that organizations with sufficient resources can now easily and cheaply procure innumerable terabytes of data. Today's competitive advantage lies in the ability to sift through all this data, select relevant information, assess its accuracy and completeness, and then synthesize it in ways that are insightful and conducive to decision-making.

Our second challenge, which can't be alleviated by the overwhelming amount of data already at our fingertips, is timeless: more often than not, truly valuable information is not readily available. The fight for this intelligence is generally a zero-sum game. Our adversaries are keenly aware of this fact and often go to extraordinary lengths to derail our efforts while creating an informational edge for themselves. They may embark on their own fight for risk intelligence. They may try to actively prevent us from obtaining pertinent information. They may try to misdirect us through deliberate deception and misinformation campaigns. Or they may fortify vulnerabilities and then go on the offensive in order to make us shift resources to defensive activities.

As British war historian Major General J. F. C. Fuller famously noted, "the true general is the creator quite as much as the applier of knowledge." From this perspective, shaping and personally spearheading the fight for risk intelligence is an essential role and responsibility of senior leaders.[73] It is they who must determine priorities for intelligence gathering—based on the assessment of the information needed to shape strategy, manage risk and direct execution. Senior leaders may conclude, for example, that not knowing certain facts about the environment or adversaries poses an unacceptable risk. This, in turn, may lead to a greater willingness to put resources, and in some domains, even lives, at risk in order to obtain information that is adequately complete and reliable.

While we have used the term "fighting for risk intelligence" metaphorically, we should note that sometimes, procuring mission-critical information is a literal fight. When preparing and conducting a military campaign, important resources will be committed to uncover vulnerabilities, opportunities and potential threats. Before staging a full-scale rescue operation, firefighters may put their lives at risk to further evaluate the nature of an emergency incident and the danger it may pose to citizens, communities and their colleagues. As with other forms of strategic calculus, the amount of risk decision makers are willing to take reflects the importance and urgency of the missing intelligence.

To ensure the fight is adequately rigorous, the leader's informational assessment—which the US military refers to as Priority Intelligence Requirements—must be continually updated, widely distributed and clearly explained. The empowerment to the edges of the organization to fight for risk intelligence must be enabled by granting authority and providing resources and guidance. A clear directive to look for the surprising or unexpected must also be conveyed, because seemingly benign signals, often seen only by those in the trenches, may be a sign of important environmental changes ahead. As a result, staying on alert and actively fighting for risk intelligence becomes everyone's responsibility, a standard of excellence, and a prevailing mindset and culture.

This philosophy is exemplified by a unified structure at the top of the US military's chain of command. Five four-star Geographic Combatant Commanders are resourced explicitly to conduct the fight for risk intelligence in their assigned Theaters of Operations. They study adversaries and competitors to the national security interests, develop plans, build networks of capabilities and relationships, and work closely with allies. All of this sets the advantageous environmental conditions and give US forces the necessary understanding and the latticework of capabilities to be agile. Chuck served as Geographic Combatant Commander in his combined duties as Commander of NORAD and US Northern Command, defending the homeland and North America.

The task of fighting for risk intelligence is getting more complex every day. Advances in technology—including cyber espionage and reconnaissance systems, both visual and electronic—are making it easier for our adversaries to conduct their intelligence gathering while detecting and disrupting ours.[74] Social media is enabling progressively sophisticated deception and weaponization of information. Meanwhile, as we'll explore more fully in the following chapters, the proliferation of the "post-truth" societal culture,[75] where evidence becomes secondary to emotions and beliefs, is impairing reasoned inquiry and debate within organizations. All of these challenges must be confronted head-on.

What's On Our Radar Screen?

If done right, the fight for risk intelligence will produce a wealth of useful information. But as anyone who has labored through multi-hundred-page executive and board packages filled with memos, tables and charts knows, synthesizing all this data and meaningfully connecting the dots can be very challenging. This experience reflects what psychologists and behavioral economists have known for some time: we humans have significant difficulties making overarching decisions based on large numbers of disjointed pieces of information. Worse yet, we are at risk of arriving at dramatically different conclusions if some of the data changes slightly or is presented differently.

When we view organizations as dynamic portfolios of risks, we realize that a system for identifying, monitoring and actively managing this portfolio can become a powerful way to synthesize and intuitively present relevant information and establish a common language and knowledge base. In this section, we present the concept of an organizational *risk radar* to illustrate how such a system (which would be referred to as the *assessment board* in the US military) can be implemented in practice. While we have found risk radars helpful across different types of organizations, their practical implementations range from highly quantitative to largely qualitative. What matters most is the discipline of identifying the relevant portfolio of risks and uncertainties; developing processes that detect environmental changes and assess their ramifications; and creating a bias for action grounded in rigorous governance, preparedness, and planning.

The risk radar we created for a well-known financial institution some years ago illustrates a quantitative version of our approach. The figure below shows that on a 30,000-foot level, the firm is exposed to financial, operational, strategic, cybersecurity and a number of other risks. Additionally, its operations, balance sheet and competitiveness are subject to several different types of uncertainty, including advances in technology (in this firm's case, AI and robotics) and geopolitical and macroeconomic environments (in this firm's case, global trade). With respect to different types of risk depicted on the radar, the sizes of the circles indicate their potential financial impact,[76] colors indicate whether they are within the firm's tolerance for risk,[77] and placement depicts an assessment of the firm's preparedness to manage these types of threats in real time, with closer proximity to the center indicating greater readiness.

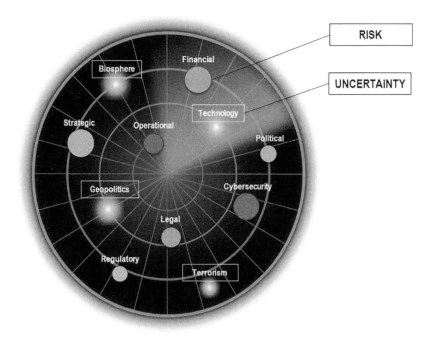

Organizational Risk Radar

Despite its seeming simplicity, a risk radar can incorporate vast amounts of data, quantitative analyses and qualitative assessments. The version presented here extends the best practices in risk management and strategy in three important ways. First, it carefully delineates between risk and uncertainty, creating separate processes for assessing, monitoring and managing these very different types of exposures. Second, its design explicitly reflects the types of decisions we expect will be made based on this information. Third, it fosters an organizational bias for action by integrating surveillance and risk assessments with governance, planning and explicit risk ownership.

As we discussed in Chapter 4, even dealing with well understood risks in practice entails complex decision-making under uncertainty. Using financial risk as an example, the following figure illustrates how risk radars can put a wealth of information at our fingertips and establish a direct path from our judgments to operational processes.

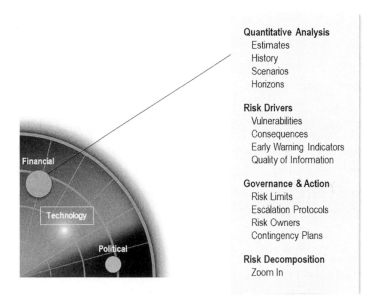

Assessing, Monitoring, and Managing Risk

The figure shows that for a risk analysis to be comprehensive, it must reflect the fact that our organization's portfolio of risks may entail entirely different threats and opportunities in different environments. The same set of vulnerabilities may present a totally acceptable risk during a period of tranquility but threaten the firm's viability in a crisis, when volatility spikes and financial markets start moving in tandem.[78] More often than not, however, our operating landscapes and our portfolio of risks evolve in parallel.

These different moving parts, internal and external, can be effectively deconstructed, analyzed, and coupled with early warning indicators of risk.[79]

As mentioned before, risks depicted on the radar can be color coded to indicate their adherence to our organization's risk tolerance, which is the first step in linking the process of monitoring and assessment to governance and action. A risk appearing on the radar in green would indicate that it's well within our risk tolerance. If due to an environmental shift or changes in our internal circumstances a risk transitions from green to yellow, this would signify that the first tier of risk limits has been breached. Crossing the next two, increasingly serious tiers of risk limits would lead to the risk being displayed in orange and red, respectively.

For each tier of risk limits, the radar system can be programmed to issue formal notifications, request additional analyses, or require formal meetings and documented decisions.[80] At some companies, a breach of a red risk limit may force an automatic risk mitigation action. When risk limits and formal escalation protocols are coupled with explicit risk ownership and extensive contingency planning, organizations develop a bias for deliberate action that enables them to mitigate threats and capture opportunities in real time.

Of course, actively managing risk in practice requires the ability to switch back and forth between aggregate risks and their very granular drivers, akin to the "zoom in/zoom out" capability of advanced military radars. As shown in the following figure, financial risks can be subdivided into market, credit and funding risks. In turn, market risks can be further broken into equity, interest rate, liquidity, currency and commodity risks, while credit can be broken into default and credit spread risk.[81] For example, if an organization's overall financial risk jumps from green to orange, the executive team can quickly zero in on the risks that have experienced the greatest increase in order to prioritize action. This process can be replicated across organizational levels, so that increasingly granular risks and opportunities are identified, assessed, monitored, governed and acted upon by the accountable and empowered decision makers.

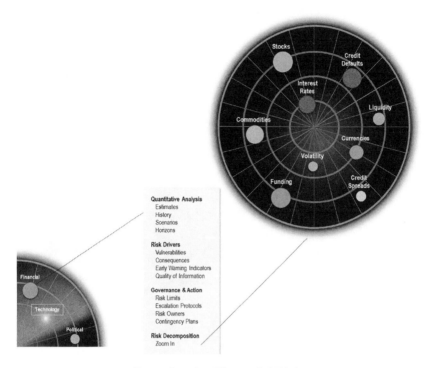

Zooming In: Financial Risk

Penetrating Uncertainty

A risk radar is an early warning and management system that helps organizations detect, asses and respond to changes in circumstances. These may encompass environmental changes, such as economic cycles or disruptive competitors, as well as our own activities, such as mergers and acquisitions, the launch of new products, balance sheet restructurings and business model transformations. The radar enables us to capture and effectively surveil the net result of the complex interactions of these external and internal drivers. It becomes especially powerful when it can properly differentiate between risk and uncertainty and create separate processes for monitoring and managing their attendant threats and opportunities. In order to do that, it must recognize that uncertainty cannot be measured quantitatively because it encompasses situations where the range of possible outcomes and their like-lihoods are unknowable.

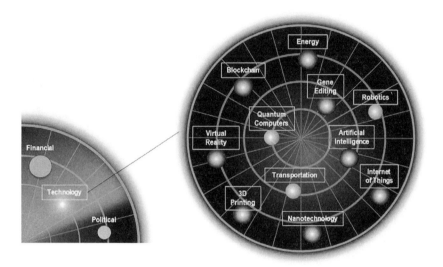

Areas of Uncertainty in Technology

Most organizations face several major classes of uncertainty, including technology, geopolitics, biosphere and terrorism.[82] As with risks, each type of uncertainty can be broken into meaningful subcomponents, with technology, for example, encompassing artificial intelligence, gene editing, robotics, transportation, energy and others. Understanding these rapidly advancing fields requires a great deal of specialized knowledge. With the help of domain experts, organizations can fight for risk intelligence by continuously surveilling the relevant developments. On an ongoing basis, they can visualize a wide range of future scenarios and assess attendant vulnerabilities, consequences, key thresholds and potential actions.[83]

As we emphasized in Chapter 4, the future will undoubtedly end up being different from our scenarios, and the actions we'll end up taking will undoubtedly be different from pre-existing contingency plans. But the act of planning will foster agility—by improving our understanding of the environment and positioning us to recognize change. When technology advances cross key thresholds (an analog of risk limits) relevant to our organizations, our escalation protocols would set in motion early interventions, spur a fight for additional risk intelligence or activate strategic plans. A few publicly available examples will ground this explanation of the process in specifics.

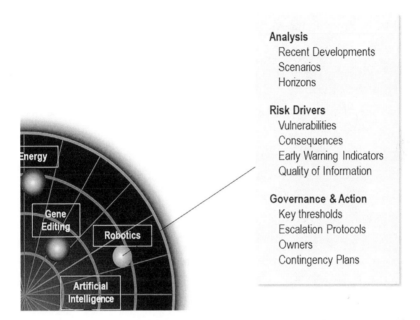

Analysis
Recent Developments
Scenarios
Horizons

Risk Drivers
Vulnerabilities
Consequences
Early Warning Indicators
Quality of Information

Governance & Action
Key thresholds
Escalation Protocols
Owners
Contingency Plans

Penetrating Uncertainty

In geopolitics, "space as a new battlefield" is an area of uncertainty that has long been actively studied and monitored by the US military establishment. An attack on missile-warning systems or on GPS and commercial communication satellites would pose a significant threat to the national interests and security. The detonation of a nuclear weapon in low earth orbit or the upper atmosphere (the so-called EMP attack) could cause widespread devastation of electric grids, critical infrastructure, satellites, air traffic control, and military and civilian communication systems. Once the relevant factors—including the rival states' advances in hypersonic aircraft and ballistic missiles technologies—reached a critical mass, they triggered a 2018 proposal to create a new military branch—the US Space Force—dedicated to the development of the next generation of space warfighting capabilities.[84]

In the realm of biosphere developments, lacking preparedness to pandemics is a significant vulnerability, as illustrated by the 2014 outbreak of Ebola in the US. After a number of individuals who traveled to the country were diagnosed with the virus and several US medical professionals were infected, a wide range of frantic actions had to be devised and put in place in real time. They included the appointment of a national coordinator, the creation of rapid response teams, airport screenings and mandatory quarantines. Simply put, Ebola was not on the radar screens of the relevant stakeholders, such as the Centers for Disease Control, in ways conducive to agility. If it were, the rapid spread of the disease on the western coast of Africa several months prior to the outbreak in the US would have set in motion a range of protective and preventive activities.

Now consider a technology change. Quantum computers use principles of quantum physics to operate on data exponentially faster than existing computers. By breaking encryptions used by governments, companies, armed forces, and financial markets and potentially penetrating payment and record-keeping systems, quantum computers may eventually threaten the stability of economic, financial and national security systems. If this rapidly developing area of technology is placed on the radar screens of government officials, regulators and organizations, they can continually assess threats and opportunities as quantum computers become increasingly powerful. A change in encryption protocols may need to be enacted when quantum computing crosses certain key technological thresholds.

Also in technology, the eventual impact of gene editing on medicine, healthcare and agriculture is likely to be profound. Groundbreaking new methods are already used to correct disease-causing gene mutations in human embryos and create pandemic-resistant animals and plants. Future applications may be even more transformative: using gene-based therapies to cure diseases such as cancer, growing human organs inside of animals or in labs, or eradicating infectious diseases by altering or eliminating entire species of insects.[85] Among its many promises, gene editing may lead to an increase in population-level longevity. If advances in gene editing cross certain key thresholds, a variety of organizations in the public and private sectors will need to take decisive action to address their exposures to this environmental shift.

Connecting the Dots

Developing and effectively using risk radars requires a specific collective skillset and a well-crafted organizational division of labor. Conceptualizing vulnerabilities and consequences requires a keen understanding of both the operating environment and the organization's strategy and business model. Quantifying risks across scenarios and time horizons requires expertise in data analysis, financial modeling and risk management. Defining meaningful forward-looking early warning indicators requires a deep knowledge of economics, financial markets, and business strategy and a great deal of practical experience. Surveilling broad areas of uncertainty requires domain expertise in geopolitics and economics, technology, biosphere and terrorism.[86] Throughout, success rests on the collaboration and mutual education of business and data analysts, financial modelers, risk managers, operating executives and senior leaders.

Success also rests on the organizational ability to connect the dots across a multitude of capabilities, skillsets, languages and silos, which requires a concerted effort. We've seen it done through two dominant approaches. One, which is used, for instance, by the US National Counterterrorism Center (NCTC) in the realm of national security, brings together a variety of specialized experts to exchange and assess information and shape solutions. The other approach involves dedicated staff responsible for synthesizing information across multiple disciplines. Playing this role requires special education and experience as well as the ability to speak different technical languages. The elite Talpiot program in the Israeli army is an example of this approach in the realm of innovation. Talpiot soldiers usually earn advanced degrees in physics, aeronautics or computer science—all while undergoing field training with all major branches of the defense forces. This gives them a unique ability to break through intellectual and organizational silos and develop creative solutions to seemingly intractable problems.

As both military and corporate leaders can attest, watching radar screens is an exercise in extremes. Generally, long periods of relative tranquility are suddenly interrupted by a threat, leading to frantic activity. This presents a difficult leadership challenge: keeping team members—across the organization and out to its very edges—alert and ready for action at a moment's notice. Ongoing education, training and war games play an important role. Equally critical is the cultural and leadership setting that creates a strong shared purpose and keeps the whole organization engaged even during mundane periods—because everyone feels a sense of ownership of the job of fighting for risk intelligence.

The Risk Levers of Agility

Some time ago, before we met, Leo had an intriguing conversation with a prominent NATO commander. It used to be the case, the commander remarked, that military strategy would be shaped and, as it was being executed, a strategic communication campaign would be launched to explain the rationale and get various stakeholders on board. In the world of social media and instantaneous transmission of information, he stressed, a very different approach is required. An evaluation of how various military actions may be received by the global public must be integrated into the strategic calculus from the beginning. This, at times, fundamentally changes the entire strategy.

This example provides a useful parallel to the traditional relationship between corporate strategy and risk management—and ways in which it must be enhanced to foster agility. In pursuit of stated objectives, companies evaluate the available resources and design a set of initiatives and transactions. If best practices are followed, these actions are analyzed on a forward-looking basis, both in terms of their stand-alone risks and their potential impact on the organization's overall portfolio of risks. If risks are deemed acceptable, plans are carried out. Otherwise, strategic calculus is used to mitigate risks, increase the risk-bearing capacity or readjust the objectives.

This proven way to keep organizations safe and sound is *not* what we mean by the active management of portfolios of risks. In fact, this sequential "goals->activities->risks" process gives us a rather limited control: our portfolio of risks remains a *side-effect* of business, financial and operational decisions; and we only rebalance it when we must mitigate risks that are excessive. As a result, we are unable to answer some fundamental questions:

- "Are we taking the appropriate *total amount* of risk—that is not excessive but also not inadequate—in pursuit of our goals?"

- "Are we taking the right *types of risks*?" and

- "Is our portfolio of risks an "optimal" way to achieve objectives in the current environment?"[87]

Consider a complementary approach originally pioneered in finance and later successfully applied in other domains:

1. Use strategic calculus to determine our organization's overall *risk appetite*—the total amount of risk we are willing to take in pursuit of our objectives and able to bear given our financial and organizational capacity.

2. Explicitly construct the desired portfolio of risks using what is known as a risk budgeting process. Given the "business we are in" and our views on competitive landscapes, economies and financial markets, determine how risk appetite should be allocated across different types of risk.

3. Design a set of initiatives and transactions that best position us to achieve stated objectives given our risk appetite and the desired portfolio of risks.

If we follow this approach, an environmental shift or a change in our own circumstances—detected by our radar—will force us to re-evaluate our risk appetite, our portfolio of risks and our business activities.

This process is best illustrated by describing how some companies and investors navigate economic cycles. When they believe an economic recovery is likely to begin, with both business and market conditions improving, they may increase the firm's risk appetite and position operations, balance sheets and asset portfolios to benefit from an increase in both interest rates and stock prices and a decline in both market volatility and corporate defaults. The amount of risk allocated to each of these systematic risk types will be dictated by a multitude of considerations, including the relative risk/return attractiveness of various business and financial opportunities. Conversely, an anticipation of a recession, companies and investors may reduce their risk appetite and rebalance their portfolios of risks to benefit from a decline in both interest rates and stock prices and an increase in volatility and corporate defaults.

Risk appetite is one of the most powerful levers at the disposal of leadership teams. It must be continually dialed to just the right level—to reflect our overarching objectives and our capacity to withstand the potential negative consequences of risk. In practice, however, it is often seen merely as a big-picture leadership communication and culture formation tool—similar to an organization's mission and vision. In typical corporate parlance, risk appetite helps set the "tone at the top" and shape general attitudes toward risk-taking, safety and soundness.

More often than not, risk appetite is defined as a large collection of disjointed individual risks that range from market share losses and earnings shortfalls to balance sheet metrics, credit ratings and reputational exposures. For large and complex organizations, this can involve hundreds of line items. While such a process looks comprehensive and tends to appease regulators and governance experts, it has proven wholly impractical and ineffective for strategic decision-making and in fostering agility. In our experience, companies that define risk appetite in this way are usually unable to perform a rigorous strategic calculus, actively manage their portfolios of risks or convincingly demonstrate that their risk appetite is aligned with their stated objectives.

In order to achieve agility, risk appetite must be defined in a way that is practically useful: custom-tailored to the organization's business model, operating philosophy and the expectation of how the portfolio of risks will be managed over time. For example, if the leadership team believes that dynamically adjusting and allocating the risk appetite is an important aspect of the "business they are in," then the risk appetite framework and the attendant analytical and IT infrastructure must be designed accordingly. In our experience with leading companies and investors, an effective combination of quantitative and qualitative tools can be used to make this achievable.[88]

By recognizing that our organization's portfolios of risks can be explicitly constructed and proactively rebalanced, we equip ourselves with a set of powerful levers: the total risk appetite, the portfolio of risks and the risk equations of underlying individual risks that can be separately altered. As we'll discuss more fully in Chapter 10, this paves the way to execution dexterity: the ability to holistically and dynamically deploy all risk, business, and organizational levers, individually and in combinations, as environments change. In contrast, when we use conventional approaches that make our portfolio of risks a side effect of other decisions, we deprive ourselves of strategic and financial flexibility and impair our ability to achieve goals, mitigate threats and seize opportunities through agility.

Two Modes of the Agility Process

Environmental changes in need of detection, assessment and response fall into two distinct categories. The first category consists of events that afford organizations adequate time to go through the full Agility Process in real time, as things unfold. For example, in the late 1990s, some asset managers became concerned about the astronomical valuations of Internet companies and equity markets at large. They concluded, as Robert Shiller did in *Irrational Exuberance*, that stock prices were unsustainable. Recognizing the dangers, and futility of trying to predict when or if a market correction would take place, these investors put their entire organizations on alert and devoted significant effort to evaluating potential offensive and defensive actions across a wide range of scenarios. When the Dotcom bubble started to burst in March 2000, they sprang into action, activating the initial set of strategies designed to benefit from a market sell-off. From March 2000 to October 2002, as Nasdaq fell over 75 percent, they carried on the iterative process of close monitoring, continuous reassessment and multifaceted response, significantly outperforming less agile competitors. Similarly, organizations that will end up successfully navigating the ongoing industrial revolution will continually monitor relevant risks and uncertainties and identify new ones, assess implications and potential actions in various scenarios, and be prepared to decisively act when the time is right.

The second category is comprised of events that happen virtually instantaneously, depriving organizations of the time to react or control over the events. Certain types of terrorist and military attacks, natural disasters, financial shocks, corporate bankruptcies and political coups belong to this category, with notable historical examples including the "Black Monday" stock market crash (1987), Russia's sovereign default (1998), the Deepwater Horizon oil spill (2010) and the Fukushima nuclear disaster. Surviving such dislocations requires risk intelligence and resilience: organizations must be able to identify and assess potentially lethal vulnerabilities and then develop and execute on a set of protective and preventive measures that will allow them to bounce back from adversity. In other words, they must go through the "detect, assess, and respond" Agility Process, but with one important caveat: after the detection and assessment, instead of waiting for the event to occur and being ready to respond in real time, they must mitigate their risks (i.e., change their risk equations) *in advance*. This is precisely why, as we mentioned in Chapter 3, resilience is both a mission-critical aspect and an outcome of agility.

Take the case of NFL concussions. Because they happen instantaneously and provide no opportunity for real time risk mitigation, the corresponding risk equation must be altered in advance. After the NFL concluded that this systematic risk must be actively managed, a number of risk management strategies were deployed. They included helmet engineering advancements (protection that reduces the players' vulnerability), helmet-hit and other game rule changes (deterrence that reduces the likelihood of concussions), and greater funding for medical and neuroscience research directed, among other things, at finding more effective post-concussion treatments (mitigation of consequences).

In another example, after long viewing flood risk as the nature of its business, the Federal Emergency Management Agency (FEMA) has determined that this exposure exceeded the agency's risk appetite. Given that many flood losses cannot be mitigated during natural disasters, in 2018 FEMA decided to alter its risk equation in advance by launching the National Flood Insurance Program that started to sell catastrophe bonds to private investors.[89]

Proactively and pre-emptively changing our risk equations—*in conjunction* with fostering our ability to respond to threats and opportunities in real time—is an especially powerful aspect of agility. When Chuck served as Commander of NORAD and US Northern Command, he was involved in a number of initiatives designed to deny the use of commercial aviation as a weapon, which was a top priority in the aftermath of the 9/11 terrorist attacks. Some of the initiatives, as described by the US Transportation Security Administration, enhanced airport security and put in place systems "to vet passengers in advance of flying,"[90] thus modifying the nation's risk equation in advance. Other programs improved the country's ability to detect, assess and mitigate threats as they occur. Both sets of measures were widely publicized, providing deterrence against future attacks.

~

Even in the presence of situational awareness and risk intelligence, we have all observed how leaders and teams can become paralyzed when confronted with an environmental change, a threat or an opportunity. To address this phenomenon, in the following three chapters we will explore organizational, cultural and leadership dimensions of agility. In this process, we'll introduce and deconstruct decisiveness—the organizational bias for deliberate action—and demonstrate how this core organizational competence that can be consistently cultivated in practice. We start by leveraging military theory and experience to describe the command-and-control doctrine conducive to agility.

CHAPTER 7

COMMAND, CONTROL AND RADICAL EMPOWERMENT

Some of the most consequential historical examples of organizational agility date back to the Napoleonic Wars (1803–1815). To confront the fog and friction of conflict that Tolstoy portrayed so well in *War and Peace*, Napoleon's Grande Armée, empowered by the liberating experience of the French Revolution, developed a highly effective command-and-control system that led to historic victories. In 1806, for example, the Prussian army suffered heavy defeats in the twin battles of Jena and Auerstedt, as recounted by historian Stephen Bungay:

> Napoleon was able to communicate very rapidly with the Marshals because they shared a basic operating doctrine, and he explained his intentions as well as what he wanted them to do. He expected them to use their initiative and act without orders in line with his intentions. They did. The result was an operational tempo which left the incredulous Prussians bewildered.[91]

As opposed to the traditional centralized and process-oriented command-and-control systems practiced by the Prussians, and most other armies at the time, the operating philosophy of the French Empire was fundamentally different. It revolved around officers up and down the command chain making independent decisions based on their understanding of Napoleon's vision and rationale. Their actions revealed, as military historian Trevor Dupuy writes in *The Evolution of Weapons and Warfare,* "complete and aggressive responsiveness" to the will of their leader, "even without orders, and miles distant."[92] This delegation of authority and responsibility to conduct operations based on quickly evolving local circumstances required a great deal of trust, as well as tolerance for the inevitable mistakes.

In the following decades, leading Prussian generals and war theorists devoted a great deal of thought to developing the new command-and-control system. The need was made more pressing by technological advances, increasing complexity and greater geographical dispersion of military campaigns. All of that made real time centralized command challenging, if not impossible. To best exploit real time opportunities and manage risk through empowered decentralized execution, the concept of *directive command* (or, in modern terms, *leading by mission*) was created.[93]

It became an essential role and responsibility of the commander to articulate his intent, explain the rationale and provide appropriate guidance as to how the objectives should be achieved. Clausewitz was integral to this effort, and the theory of war he subsequently developed comprehensively explained the fundamental nature of conflict, the dynamic drivers of risk and—based on that understanding—the directive command system necessary for battlefield agility. It was so well crafted that two hundred years later, *On War* is still taught in the US military. It has been an essential resource in the development and a continual enhancement of Mission Command.

Mission Command is both a command-and-control philosophy and an operational doctrine that melds centralized, top-down vision and planning with decentralized execution. Its primary goal, in the words of General Martin Dempsey, former Chairman of the Joint Chiefs of Staff, is to create "a continual cognitive effort to understand, adapt and to direct effectively the achievement of" stated objectives.[94] As a result, a myriad of independent actions and on-the-spot improvisations effectively deliver results "as if they are centrally coordinated." According to the US military, to successfully operationalize Mission Command, "subordinate leaders at all echelons" must "exercise disciplined initiative and act aggressively and independently to accomplish the mission."[95] It is the fundamental premise of this doctrine that organizations that practice distributed leadership in this fashion will acquire a *bias for action* and gain, in Dempsey's words, "competitive adaptability and tempo advantages" that lead to what he expressly refers to as "agility."

Mission Command is based on three key tenets: shared understanding, intent and trust. In the language of our book, shared understanding encompasses the knowledge of the environment, strategic vision, operational guidance and a decision-making framework grounded in risk intelligence. As situations rapidly evolve, leaders at all levels become keen observers and co-creators of the shared understanding as they fight for risk intelligence and adjust strategies in real time. They clearly and concisely express the purpose, specific goals, priorities and key tasks of a mission in their statements of *Commander's Intent*.

As increasingly granular statements of Commander's Intent cascade down the command chain, they help continually explain to the entire organization what must be achieved and why. In the military, the attendant operational guidance—*how* to achieve the mission—is usually kept to a minimum. The "how" in an articulation of Commander's Intent is usually referred to as "key tasks" or "method," generally describing constraints, restraints and limitations on actions. They are selected carefully so as not to unduly limit initiative and improvisation, and there is always a concerted effort to keep the list small and focused on must do's and must don'ts. Commanders are conscious of the link between risk and the level of specificity of the key tasks prescribed. The philosophy of command has a clear bias that greater specificity often entails more risk. In business and other domains, more granular operational guidance is often required. In the next chapter, we will discuss how it can be shaped and articulated at different levels of specificity, as determined by the nature of the organization's business and the operating environment.

When a commander creates or accepts a mission, he or she assumes both the authority and responsibility to act and to lead in pursuit of stated objectives.[96] The role of Commander's Intent is to establish the strategic direction, help visualize the unfolding of an operation and empower disciplined initiative. The senior leaders' ability to clearly communicate the desired end state of the mission is especially critical. By knowing what success looks like after the fog clears and the sounds of battle fade, subordinates can aggressively and creatively pursue the overarching objectives even if circumstances change, some of the tasks become unachievable and pre-existing plans fall apart.

One of the most powerful statements of Commander's Intent of all time belongs to John F. Kennedy. In his May 25, 1961, address to Congress, he stated: "this nation should commit itself to achieving the goal, before this decade is out, of landing a man on the moon and returning him safely to the Earth." The audacious vision was accompanied by an explanation of an overarching purpose: to take a leading role in space exploration and thereby capture the hearts and minds of humanity in the "battle…between freedom and tyranny." Referring to the Soviets' launch of Sputnik in 1957, President Kennedy clearly conveyed that the goal of showcasing the advanced technologies and space capabilities of the United States, saying "no single space project in this period will be more impressive to mankind." While some in the public may not have known that the mission was also seen as a means of deterrence against the Soviet Union, that was well understood in the government and military circles. But Kennedy also made clear, in stirring words, that the mission was not only a response to the Soviet achievement, saying "this is not merely a race. Space is open to us now; and our eagerness to share its meaning is not governed by the efforts of others. We go into space because whatever mankind must undertake, free men must fully share."

In stark contrast to so many proposals made by presidents in congressional addresses, the speech also detailed a set of the key tasks required as well as the financial resources Kennedy was requesting Congress to allocate. The specificity he provided merits full quotation:

We propose to accelerate the development of the appropriate lunar spacecraft. We propose to develop alternate liquid and solid fuel boosters, much larger than any now being developed, until certain which is superior. We propose additional funds for other engine development and for unmanned explorations—explorations which are particularly important for one purpose which this nation will never overlook: the survival of the man who first makes this daring flight. But in a very real sense, it will not be one man going to the moon—if we make this judgment affirmatively, it will be an entire nation. For all of us must work to put him there.

Secondly, an additional 23 million dollars, together with 7 million dollars already available, will accelerate development of the Rover nuclear rocket. This gives promise of some day providing a means for even more exciting and ambitious exploration of space, perhaps beyond the moon, perhaps to the very end of the solar system itself.

Third, an additional 50 million dollars will make the most of our present leadership, by accelerating the use of space satellites for world-wide communications.

Fourth, an additional 75 million dollars—of which 53 million dollars is for the Weather Bureau—will help give us at the earliest possible time a satellite system for world-wide weather observations.[97]

This degree of strategic and operational clarity of direction is essential to agility. Without it, the unity of effort and the effectiveness of decentralized execution are not achievable—irrespective of the organization's competitive advantages, unique capabilities or the motivation of the employees.[98]

Top Brain, Bottom Brain

The requirements for fostering the continual cognitive process of detecting, assessing and responding to change have been illuminated by recent discoveries in neuroscience. Scientists have learned that while the workings of the human brain are enormously complex, a fundamental division can be drawn between what they refer to as the top brain and the bottom brain systems. These systems are distinct in their anatomy, neurological connections and cognitive functions.[99] According to many scientific studies, the top portions of the brain are largely responsible for making decisions, as well as devising, carrying out and adjusting plans. The bottom portions of the brain are largely involved in classifying and making sense of what one perceives. In order to develop deep situational awareness, make optimal decisions and effectively execute, the two parts of the brain must collaborate constantly and closely. As the top brain creates and carries out a plan, it generates expectations about what should or could happen. This, in turn, primes and focuses the bottom brain. As the bottom brain detects and assesses the consequences of actions and environmental changes, this information is related to the top brain so it can either confirm or revise the plan.

Agile teams and organizations operate in a comparable fashion. Leaders serve the functions of the top brain, not only shaping and articulating the Commander's Intent but also spearheading the fight for risk intelligence and nurturing an environment that fosters effective decentralized execution. Subordinate leaders and their teams vigorously develop situational awareness and directly drive execution. They are encouraged and empowered to use their specialized knowledge and creativity to innovate, take smart risks and find optimal solutions for achieving goals—all within well-defined boundaries of initiative. They not only continuously monitor and assess the progress of execution and changes in the operating landscape but also promptly communicate them up the command chain so leadership teams can adjust plans and operations in as close as possible to real time.

Such a rich and balanced communication and collaboration between organizational top and bottom brain teams is fostered by what we call a priming-education-feedback process. In our discussions of this imperative, Admiral Dennis Blair, former Director of National Intelligence, offered an illustration of such priming. The intelligence community is most effective in fighting for risk intelligence when, in addition to constantly looking for the unexpected, it is continually primed by senior government and military officials about their priorities, goals and concerns. The inverse process is equally important. As General Michael Hayden, former Director of CIA and NSA, has stressed to us, the intelligence community must devote concerted effort to deeply understanding how political leaders process information, conceptualize the environment, and use data and analytical tools. Only then will intelligence agencies be effective in educating political leaders on the meaning of relevant signals and developments.

The proactive nature of agility, with its inherent bias for deliberate action and the will to win, dictates how organizational top and bottom brains must function beyond the exchange of information. The Theory of Cognitive Modes, originally developed by cognitive scientist Stephen Kosslyn and subsequently applied to organizations by Stephen and Leo, provides a useful framework.[100] Kosslyn identifies four primary cognitive dispositions that influence people's decision-making and behavior: *adaptor, stimulator, perceiver* and *mover*. He points out that while people always use both the top and bottom parts of the brain, they differ in the degree to which they utilize each *above and beyond* what is dictated by immediate circumstances. For example, when nothing in the environment may be forcing us to go beyond routine activities, some people may be more inclined to proactively create a plan for capitalizing on a potential opportunity. In contrast, others in the same situation may be habitually more vigorous in applying their bottom brain skills to continually enhance situational awareness. Cognitive modes apply to organizations as well, helping illuminate their business models, successes and failures as well as conditions for agility.

The *adaptor* mode arises when people do not deeply utilize either the top or the bottom brain. Those operating in this mode are typically not overly concerned with formulating plans, nor are they focused on classifying and interpreting what they experience. Instead, they tend to be absorbed by immediate imperatives and tasks, allowing external forces to mold their actions and results.

In the realm of organizations, Citigroup circa 2007 is a perfect example. We've alluded earlier to the famous statement by the firm's top brain (Chairman and CEO Charles Prince), "When the music stops, in terms of liquidity, things will be complicated. But as long as the music is playing, you've got to get up and dance."[101] In fact, Prince was keenly aware of the vicious cycles we described in Chapter 5. He knew that Citigroup was taking progressively larger amounts of risk in the build-up to the crisis, but he refused to pull back: the firm could not afford to forgo earnings or lose market shares. Mimicking the behaviors of reckless competitors is an antithesis of agility and a hallmark of adaptors who lack strategic vision. But Prince also knew that when the vicious cycle of deleveraging eventually starts, buyers ("liquidity") will disappear and it will become impossible to mitigate risk in real time.

To make matters worse, Citigroup's portfolio of risks was obscured by a multitude of disparate processes and systems, leaving the firm's bottom brains without a context necessary for developing situational awareness and being on the lookout for threats. In the words of one of Lewis Carroll's characters, "if you don't know where you are going, any road can take you there." For Citigroup, a sitting duck with deactivated top and bottom brains, that road led to a taxpayer bailout.

The *stimulator* mode arises when people deeply utilize the top brain but not the bottom brain. Operating in this mode can be vital to generating creative ideas and solutions, but without the balance of the situational awareness from the bottom brain, strategies can be excessively risky and disconnected from reality. This mode can also lead to an inability to change plans when an environmental shift warrants a strategy adjustment.

The course of the Korean War was fundamentally altered when General Douglas MacArthur failed to assess numerous bottom-brain warnings—signals from the battlefield, diplomatic channels and advice based on historical precedents—that the People's Republic of China had the capacity and intention to intervene. A few years earlier, German commanders similarly refused to listen to subordinates and acknowledge the reality on the ground during the battle for Stalingrad, profoundly affecting the course of World War II.

In a business case in point, the demise of MF Global was precipitated by risky market bets taken by CEO Jon Corzine, who was repeatedly warned by risk managers and other executives that the firm was taking on excessive risk. As a result, as we discussed in Chapter 5, a company widely thought of as a boring financial intermediary accumulated a portfolio of risks like that of a hedge fund. It promptly went out of business when these risks materialized.

The *perceiver* mode arises when people deeply utilize the bottom brain but not the top brain. People operating in this mode focus on proactively making sense of their environment, interpreting experience, putting information in context and understanding the implications of what they encounter. That's all good, but the problem when it comes to agility is that people who operate in this mode don't devote much time to planning or developing expertise in executing on plans.

Organizations that operate in a perceiver mode are easy to spot: their senior leaders de facto outsource strategic vision and planning to organizational silos. The danger, of course, is that these silos—that are unaware of the organization's entire portfolio of risks, risk-bearing capacity or each other's activities—may end up taking interconnected risks that prove lethal. Equally importantly, while each of these silos may be staffed with exceptional people and effective in achieving its own goals, the net result may not amount to a coherent campaign that delivers on the firm's overarching objectives. As the case study of the Vietnam War in Chapter 9 will illustrate, perceiver organizations run the risk of winning lots of battles but losing the war.

The *mover* mode arises when people deeply utilize both top and bottom brain systems. They formulate and act on plans using the top brain—and also register the consequences of their actions using the bottom brain, leading to good situational awareness and effective readjustment of goals and plans.

Organizations that operate in the mover mode are positioned for agility. Their Commander's Intent is fully shaped and clearly communicated.

Actively monitored environmental signals flow up and down the command chain, leading to timely strategic and tactical readjustments. The organizational design, feedback loops and leadership communication of movers are custom-tailored to the nature of their portfolio of risks. As a result, their top and bottom brains fulfill their respective roles, effectively communicating and collaborating in pursuit of clearly defined and rigorously measured shared objectives. The case study of how Goldman Sachs navigated the global financial crisis of 2008–09 that we develop throughout the book is an illustration of the mover mode of operation.

In their book *Top Brain, Bottom Brain*, Kosslyn and G. Wayne Miller argue that for individuals, none of the cognitive modes is inherently superior to the others and that switching modes is beneficial in different situations. If we're in a meeting in which a course of action is being intensively debated, for example, we might benefit from switching to perceiver mode so that we're open-minded enough about differing views being expressed.

Just like people tend to have a dominant cognitive mode, organizations can develop one as well. For an organization to be agile, the mover mode of operation must *always* dominate, which requires an explicit choice and a concerted effort by the senior leaders. In order to detect environmental changes faster than our adversaries and proactively seize opportunities and mitigate threats, the whole organization must be fully engaged. Both top and bottom brains must habitually go above and beyond of what is minimally required, even in times that aren't clearly presenting urgent challenges.[102]

Local Knowledge

During the 1970 Apollo 13 mission to the Moon, an oxygen tank explosion crippled the service module, leading to the loss of heat in the cabin as well as power and water shortages. However, it was the damage to the spacecraft's carbon dioxide removal system that posed the most imminent danger. In a striking scene from the 1995 movie *Apollo 13*, NASA engineers gather all the things available to the astronauts in space and throw them on a table.

Using duct tape, plastic containers, tube socks, the cover of the flight plan and flight suit hoses, they create a "scrubber" device that removes the carbon dioxide from of the cabin. Using their design and guidance, the crew replicates the contraption in space and returns safely to Earth.

"Many of the engineers who created a life-saving device for Apollo 13 were among the original designers of the spacecraft," notes Major General John Barry, who headed the Space Shuttle Columbia accident investigation. "They knew its every nook and cranny, and that is what enabled them to create an effective solution in real time. In contrast, people who deemed the damage to the Columbia Shuttle non-threatening didn't have the same deep *local knowledge* as the engineers who saved Apollo 13."

In discussions on the benefits of decentralized execution, we often focus on the speed of independent decision-making. In complex, dispersed and rapidly evolving situations—especially when adversaries attempt to disrupt communications—seeking approval from superiors is both impractical and dangerous. Attempts to do so create new vulnerabilities and hamper our ability to mitigate threats and exploit opportunities.

Mission Command aims to give commanders at all levels the freedom to effectively react to rapidly changing local situations. This, among other things, is enabled by detailed local knowledge, the importance of which has been long understood and practiced by leading organizations. In marketing and branding, cross-cultural competence helps add emotional and cultural resonance to products, services and brands. Intelligence officers who run networks of informants often have an extremely detailed knowledge of the local political environment, key influencers, dialects and culture. Leaders of supermarket chains give regional managers significant latitude in determining product mixes based on the locations of the stores and the communities they serve. The impressive, ongoing innovation in the Israeli defense industry is fostered by the country's unique reserve-service system that enables reservists to develop detailed local knowledge in both the private sector and in the military. In recent years—given the vast difference in regulatory landscapes around the world—financial institutions have given their regional leaders much greater authority over investment and business decisions.

In addition to leveraging deep local knowledge, effective empowerment to the very edges of the organization requires all team members to clearly understand the boundaries within which they are expected to exercise bold initiative.

Boundaries of Initiative

For decentralized execution to work well, leaders and team members at all levels must have an appropriate freedom of action. Too much latitude will interfere with controlled execution. Micromanagement will suffocate creativity and independent decision-making necessary for seizing opportunites and adjusting to rapidly unfolding conditions. Agility requires the right balance between top-down and bottom-up decision-making. This balance—the division of labor between top and bottom brains—can be expressed in terms of clearly defined boundaries within which empowered team members can exercise disciplined initiative.

The boundaries of initiative can and do vary a great deal. In some situations, it is imperative that individuals and teams carry out Commander's Intent with little room for improvisation or creativity, which calls for tighter boundaries. For example, military pilots conducting precision air strikes usually receive very specific guidance in order to minimize collateral damage. If a corporate treasurer is instructed to raise debt without significantly changing the firm's asset/liability risk profile, the set of different capital market strategies she can explore will be limited. In contrast, situations where bottom-up decisiveness and ingenuity should be maximized would warrant significantly wider boundaries. For instance, military commanders conducting a geographically dispersed counter-insurgency campaign may be given significant latitude. The same may apply to an R&D department or company, such as Google X, whose purpose is to pursue high-risk/high-return "moonshot" solutions to intractable problems.[103]

Clearly, acceptable boundaries of disciplined initiative can vary significantly across different organizations, different parts of an organization or across different initiatives, reflecting the nature of business, the prevailing environment and specific objectives. They may also need to be altered as an organization evolves. A military invasion, a highly centralized endeavor, may be followed by stabilization operations that may be comparatively decentralized. As a startup technology company moves out of the R&D and into product commercialization stages, it may need to create a more elaborate leadership structure, and some boundaries may need to be tightened.

Across domains, empowerment and the attendant boundaries of initiative are usually established through a three-pronged approach: 1) delegation of formal authority, 2) resource allocation, and 3) risk management. Authority deals with the types of decisions that leaders and teams are allowed to make independently. Resource allocation involves the allotment of capital, human talent and organizational bandwidth to lines of business or initiatives. In business, risk limits are commonly used as an additional layer of control, while in the US military, key tasks are often accompanied by a description of constraints, restraints, and limitations.

~

To become agile, organizations must develop a capacity to dial the degree of centralization/decentralization to the right level as circumstances evolve. In order to achieve that, they must possess the mechanisms for changing the boundaries of initiative systematically and explicitly, which often entails providing the operational guidance that goes beyond what not to do. These mechanisms must be both comprehensive and flexible, so they can be custom-tailored to the unique features and circumstances of any organization. We next introduce one such mechanism that we have developed.

CHAPTER 8

OPERATIONALIZED STRATEGIC VISION

We once asked two senior executives of a well-known financial services firm to describe how their organization created long-term value. The COO's reply was entirely client-centric: her company was in the business of helping clients achieve their financial objectives. By implication, the clients' needs largely determined the firm's products, business mix and the portfolio of risks. By contrast, the CFO's reply was entirely balance sheet-centric: the firm was in the business of dynamically allocating capital to activities and markets that offered the most attractive risk-adjusted returns. While client relationships certainly were an important driver of growth and profitability, the firm's products and services were a means to an end: growing the business and delivering superior returns to shareholders. Needless to say, such differing views on the most fundamental aspects of the organization's business did not engender a unity of effort and a bias for action.

Most senior leaders devote a concerted effort to explaining the over-arching purpose and goals of their organizations and the business they are in. This is typically done through corporate mission, vision and values statements; strategic plans; and inspirational leadership communications. And yet, more often than not, team members remain uncertain what the firm's overarching strategy and business philosophy are, what they mean in concrete operational terms and how to parlay them into daily activities. This lack of clarity impairs initiative and creativity and leads to risk aversion, with even seemingly empowered executives often feeling the need to seek approval for relatively mundane decisions.

To foster agility, any organization must be able to comprehensively shape and articulate its vision and strategy, describe the business it is in, express its business philosophy and provide specific guidance with respect to appropriate behaviors, practices and boundaries of initiative up and down the command chain. The *Operationalized Strategic Vision* (OSV) process we developed addresses this need.

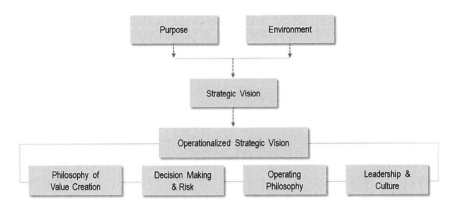

The Operationalized Strategic Vision Process

Philosophy of Value Creation

How does our organization create long-term value? Comprehensively answering this question is vital for achieving the strategic and operational clarity necessary for the unity of effort and effective decentralized execution. In addition to establishing common understanding of purpose and vision up and down the command chain and defining the business an organization is in, this is a valuable opportunity to uncover areas of ambiguity, sharply question assumptions, and reconcile beliefs and reality.

For example, in the corporate world, it is not unusual for a leadership team to start this conversation by stating that their company creates long-term value and stays relevant by fulfilling and anticipating customer needs, steadily growing businesses and earnings, driving operational efficiency and excellence, and providing superior client service. But what does this mean exactly? How do we define relevance to customers and other stakeholder groups? What is the role of innovation and risk-taking in our business model? Do we base decisions on accounting and statutory metrics that obscure the economic reality? In an effort to avoid earnings volatility disliked by Wall Street analysts, would we ever allow short-term considerations to hamper long-term performance?

Companies that strive for enduring relevance and superior performance devote a concerted effort to comprehensively articulating their philosophy of value creation. They explain how they strike the right balance between internally driven purpose and strategy and externally driven customer needs and competitive factors. They instruct employees to use economic reality as a basis for decision-making, and they work hard to instill a mindset that focuses on capturing opportunities, not just mitigating threats.

When one of the key goals of the OSV process is to foster agility, other facets of long-term value creation become important: a concerted fight for risk intelligence, active management of the portfolio of risks and creation of an environment that facilitates decentralized execution. Interestingly, given the uncertainty and volatility of the operating environment, some companies have begun describing crisis management as an integral part of their value creation, a core competence and a unique value proposition. To them, crisis management is a forward-looking and ongoing evaluation and proactive management of risk equations we described at the end of Chapter 6, as opposed to a surge of activities directed at containing damage and managing public relations after the fact.[104]

Consider the following publicly available example that we'll return to throughout this section. Since its founding in 1994, Amazon has been explicit and consistent in articulating its philosophy of value creation. It includes a relentless focus on the customer, whose interests are believed to be closely linked to the company's long-term success. The effectiveness of products and initiatives is rigorously measured, which leads to growing successful programs and discarding those that do not provide acceptable returns. As the company has stated in a number of public communications to shareholders and in public disclosures, timely and "cost-conscious" decision-making is a priority and expectation. The same applies to bold and calculated risk-taking in areas with a "sufficient probability of gaining market leadership."

To Amazon, the importance of grounding decisions in economic reality and long-term considerations is also unequivocal: "when forced to choose between optimizing the appearance of…GAAP accounting and maximizing the present value of future cash flows," the company "will take the cash flows."[105] In contrast, in a survey of 400 CFOs conducted by academic researchers and summarized by McKinsey, "fully 80 percent of CFOs…said they would reduce discretionary spending on potentially value-creating activities such as marketing and R&D in order to meet their short-term earnings targets. In addition, 39 percent said they would give discounts to customers to make purchases this quarter, rather than next, in order to hit quarterly [earnings] targets."[106] Needless to say, such practices are destructive to corporate cultures, not conducive to superior long-term performance and antithetical to agility.

Decision-Making & Risk

As core competencies, risk intelligence and decisiveness do not emerge by themselves. They become ingrained in the organizational fabric only when senior leaders position them as essential priorities and standards of excellence, and when the whole organization embraces them as such. This requires a common understanding of what it means and what it takes to be risk intelligent and decisive. The team members must also be given sufficient opportunity to learn and practice the requisite skills and capabilities.

As we discussed in Chapter 4, deliberate decisions are an outcome of strategic calculus that balances goals, risk and capacity. To ensure that a myriad of decentralized activities come together in an effective strategy implementation, senior leaders must explain in broad strokes how the strategic calculus should be performed and how risk should be identified and managed. They also must ensure the alignment and internal consistency of definitions and metrics—since goals, risks and capacity differ across organizational levels and silos. A number of years ago, as we were guiding a client through the OSV process, the company was about to go through an internal audit. Given that this process usually touches the entire organization, we asked the auditors to ask various departments and teams the following three questions. "What are your stated objectives?" "What risks do you monitor and manage?" "How do you shape decisions and evaluate alternatives, and what is the role of risk in this process?" It came as a surprise to the executive team that their top-level goals and risks—and the way they shaped decisions—were significantly disconnected from the metrics and practices down the command chain.

Amazon demonstrates how an organization can describe its decision-making framework and business philosophy. Instead of focusing on short-term profitability or stock price, Amazon has consistently pursued market leadership by using a long-term decision-making horizon. At different stages of its development—and depending on the operating environment—the firm has developed mechanisms for prioritizing certain goals (e.g., growth) over others (e.g., profitability). The discipline of consistently using strategic calculus has been reinforced by sharing the rationale behind really consequential decisions with stakeholders so they can "evaluate for themselves" whether Amazon is "making rational long-term leadership investments."

Effective strategic calculus is grounded in the deep understanding of risk, and the OSV process has proven useful in articulating how risk intelligence should be cultivated across the organization. For example, senior leaders may stress that it is everyone's responsibility to fight for risk intelligence, identify relevant risks and comprehensively assess their vulnerabilities, likelihoods and consequences. They may explicitly list the risks that have been deemed incompatible with the organization's business model or operating philosophy.[107] They may also explain how short-term and long-term objectives must be balanced and outline other broad principles, such as:

- Risk-taking must advance our strategy and priorities, must be sized according to our risk-bearing capacity, and must reflect our values and rules.

- Risk-taking must focus on the areas of our competence and have the expected return in excess of pre-defined thresholds.[108]

- When an attractive opportunity presents itself, calculated risk-taking must be bold and decisive. As the old adage says, "great poker players" (and agile organizations) "leave nothing on the table when they have a good hand."[109]

In addition to fostering a common understanding of decision-making and risk-taking, the OSV process has proven effective as a mechanism for adjusting the boundaries of initiative and dialing the decentralization to the desired level. In some cases, fairly granular boundaries of initiative may be warranted. For example, asset managers and financial services firms often impose explicit risk and size limits to constrain the risk of investments on a stand-alone basis and in terms of their impact on the portfolio of risks. The firm-wide risk appetite—and its various components stratified by risk type, lines of business or geography—can be bounded by explicit risk limits as well. Some technology and pharmaceutical companies explicitly constrain total R&D budgets as well as their allocation across individual initiatives. As Paul Zak notes in *Trust Factor*, Ritz-Carlton empowers employees to spend up to two thousand dollars to fix a problem experienced by a guest under the understanding that such expenditures will not be questioned by supervisors.[110] Ritz-Carlton appears to have concluded that the contingent liability that such empowerment creates is aligned with both the goal of creating a superior customer experience and the firm's risk-bearing capacity.

Operating Philosophy, Leadership and Culture

We "control expenses," "diligently evaluate risks," "hire carefully," and "run our business according to the highest level of morality." The behavior of our senior executives "leaves no doubt about how we feel about…the observance of rules—big or small." "We keep everyone accountable, make timely decisions and provide clients with ideas and care." We "use common sense," "treat our associates the way we would like to be treated," and deliver "high return on equity with integrity." We "will never get caught up in the hysterical optimism," and our people "will never get careless or conceited."[111] Such was the operating philosophy of Bear Stearns when it thrived under the leadership of a legendary executive and philanthropist Alan "Ace" Greenberg from late 1970s until early 1990s. That was before Ace was ousted in a coup staged by Jimmy Cayne, under whose management the firm lost the sight of the values and practices that had made it successful.

As a complement to leadership communication and organizational statements of values, the OSV process enables senior leaders to elaborate on how employees are expected to conduct affairs and interact with stakeholders. Given the diversity of business models and operational practices that can be formalized and articulated in this way, a comprehensive discussion of this topic is beyond the scope of our book. Suffice it to say that in our experience, companies have found this aspect of the OSV process useful in explaining what operational excellence means to them,[112] in framing setbacks and honest mistakes as learning opportunities, and in guiding how to measure progress and manage expenses. Given that decentralized execution requires a significant investment in training and education, using the OSV process to explain how an organization should acquire and develop human capital and cultivate the next generation of leaders has proven useful as well.

With respect to operating philosophy, as with decision-making and risk, some companies choose to explicitly describe the expected standards of behaviors and set the boundaries of initiative. For example, Ace Greenberg's demand that his associates reuse paper clips, rubber bands and inter-office-mail envelopes has become Wall Street lore. Ace explained his commitment to such rigorous expense control by frequently noting that he had "never enjoyed the smell of money burning, particularly when it is his money." In a more recent example of specific boundaries of initiative, one way Amazon aims to foster innovation is by discouraging meetings where the entire group of attendees cannot be fed by two pizzas.[113]

The organization's operating philosophy is inextricably linked to leadership and culture. No appeals to behaving ethically, taking responsibility and treating others with respect will take hold unless the leaders exemplify these standards. Environmental changes will not be detected and comprehensively assessed by employees who are disengaged or afraid that they'll be punished for bearing bad news or ridiculed for crying wolf. The entire Agility Process will break down unless it operates in a culture of empowerment, accountability and trust. We'll dedicate the following chapter to examining the specific dimensions of leadership and culture necessary for agility; many of them can be formalized and articulated through the OSV process.

In terms of its practical implementation, the OSV process, which some of our clients have described as an exercise in "corporate engineering," must be custom-tailored to the organization's culture and the personalities of senior leaders. At some firms, we have found that an executive team loves nothing more than to lock itself in a windowless room for days at a time and systematically work through the aspects of the firm's vision and philosophy that need to be fleshed out. At other firms, leaders prefer to work on these issues individually and then use a separate process to synthesize information and shape a consensus view.

Having developed a mechanism for setting the boundaries of initiative at any organization, we can now turn to the important next question: What considerations should determine the *appropriate* level of decentralization? In the process, we can examine the validity of the popular prescription that all organizations must "fearlessly decentralize" in response to accelerating change.

Why Some Flat Organizations Succeed and Others Don't

Some years ago, one of our clients—one of the world's largest investment firms—encountered a puzzling phenomenon. The firm had a clearly defined and communicated Commander's Intent: grow assets under management by delivering superior investment returns and client service. The operationalized strategic vision—values, standards of behavior and operating philosophy—was understood and consistently practiced throughout the organization. Decentralized execution was empowered, with boundaries of initiative—expressed as asset allocation and risk limits—carefully set and effectively governed. Yet the company experienced periodic bouts of significant underperformance, especially during market dislocations and crises.

In the process of assessing the drivers of losses, our attention quickly turned to the portfolios of investment risks. The company prided itself on being able to take bold, calculated risks investing in stocks, bonds and entire companies it viewed as undervalued. The decentralized execution of Commander's Intent, therefore, revolved around the selection of individual investments, whose risks were assumed to be relatively independent. In reality, however, this process accumulated a portfolio of highly interconnected (systematic) risks that all moved in unison during crises.[114] This experience led us to an important realization:

> *An organization's portfolio of risks must be a key determinant of the appropriate level of decentralization. More interconnected portfolios of risks call for greater centralization, and vice versa.*

When implementing this premise in practice, the nature of risk-taking at each organizational level must be carefully evaluated and explicitly aligned with the boundaries of initiative as they cascade down the command chain.[115] Generic prescriptions about an indiscriminate flattening of organizations in response to the Fourth Industrial Revolution are not only ineffective but outright dangerous precisely because risk must play a role in organizational design. At the same time, the critical tenet of Mission Command must also be taken to heart: boundaries of initiative must be selected very carefully so that they don't unduly limit initiative and improvisation. Micromanagement poses significant risks of its own.

The notion that a change in the organization's portfolio of risks or the external environment may warrant an adjustment in the level of decentralization brings us back to the discussion of the cognitive modes in Chapter 7. Recall that when it comes to dominant human cognitive modes—adaptor, stimulator, perceiver and mover—Stephen Kosslyn and his colleagues have argued that none of the modes are inherently superior to others and that switching modes in different situations may be beneficial. In contrast, we emphasized that for an organization to be agile, the mover mode must always dominate. Unplugging proactive and creative parts of the corporate brains is never a good idea, and both top and bottom brains must always be going above and beyond what is dictated by the immediate circumstances to detect threats and opportunities and leverage them to our advantage.

Organizations exhibit *cognitive agility* when they respond to environmental shifts by dynamically adjusting the boundaries of initiative and thus changing the level of decentralization—all while remaining in the mover mode. Agility is achieved when cognitive agility, tactical agility and strategic agility all come together.

The US military invasions of Afghanistan (2001) and Iraq (2003) started as centralized top-brain operations directed by government and military leaders. In subsequent years, as part of a comprehensive counter-insurgency strategy discussed in Chapter 5, additional combat power was brought in, and operations were decentralized to reflect the nature of a volatile and fast-changing battlefield. Missions within a single village often varied dramatically: from the clearing of terrorist cells and holding security gains through police training to building schools for girls, constructing power plants and making microloans to stimulate the economy.

Because each task required different resources and partnerships—from special force units and civilian police officers to USAID program managers—building trust within diverse teams was critical. Young officers who led those efforts had to make minute-by-minute decisions in the absence of their superiors—all while operating with a full understanding of their leaders' intent, values and tolerance for risk. The effects of these decentralized activities were monitored by senior leaders through specially designed surveillance and assessment tools. It took a great deal of courage for junior commanders to take on such immense responsibilities—and for senior leaders to relinquish control and foster an environment of trust, empowerment, and accountability.

Discussions about command-and-control philosophies, risk intelligence, strategic calculus or levels of decentralization may seem abstract. However, as part of a comprehensive intellectual and operational framework, these tools allow organizations across domains to develop and consistently practice agility, in business-as-usual environments as well as under the most dire of circumstances. Leading fire departments in the US serve as a powerful illustration.

Agility in the Fire Service

At approximately 11:40 p.m. on December 14, 2013, the Solana Cherry Creek apartment development, a 341-unit complex still under construction, burst into flames. Situated in the tree-lined Denver suburb of Glendale, the complex was surrounded by multi-story apartment buildings with hundreds of residents, many of whom had gone to sleep for the night. With the complex still in the framing stage, the wood understructure was entirely exposed and was quickly engorged in flame, turning it into a massive fireball that could be seen as far as twenty-eight miles away. Licks of flame shot up forty feet high, and the intense heat of the fire quickly radiated to the surrounding buildings. One of them began off-gassing, sending out streams of toxic smoke. Windows in several buildings began cracking. The heat was so intense that it melted the headlights, mirrors and body panels of all the cars parked alongside the complex. The whole block would soon have been consumed.

But Mark Ruzycki, Denver Fire Department's highly experienced and well-trained incident commander, the first Assistant Chief to arrive at the scene, immediately took charge. He straightaway ordered a third alarm assignment, which calls for nine engines, six trucks with aerial ladders and towers, a rescue truck, a HazMat unit, four more chiefs and a rapid intervention team. Organizing the operation according to the rigorous National Incident Management System, Ruzycki was incredibly calm as he issued commands. Having deftly assessed the full situation, he prioritized the buildings on the perimeter of the fire, where lives were in danger, rather than the inferno itself. Immediately designating each of the buildings a division of its own, he assigned each its own Division Supervisor and companies, with each company comprising four firefighters. Springing into action, each Division Supervisor then took the initiative for his structure, conducting four masterfully choreographed operations according to pre-established protocols. While some companies trained hoses on the endangered buildings, others formed rescue teams and began evacuating residents. As more engines, ladder trucks and rescue teams arrived, hoses were turned on the inferno itself. The fire was contained by 1:30 a.m., and no lives were lost.

In our most frightening and vulnerable moments—terrorist attacks, natural and man-made disasters, accidents, fires and medical emergencies— seeing firefighters arrive at the scene and spring into action reassures us that we are in good hands. Clearly, they are experienced and well-trained. They can think on their feet, deal with the unexpected and use everything at their disposal to accomplish a mission. However, often hidden from view are the key ingredients of the firefighters' agility: risk intelligence, preparedness, decisiveness and trust. As the firefighters like to remind the uninitiated, they don't just "put the wet stuff on the red stuff."

Fighting for Risk Intelligence

A fire commander's day starts when she leaves home, explains Scott Heiss, who until recently was Division Chief of Safety & Training at the Denver Fire Department. On the way, the commander registers every detail—weather, wind, humidity—trying to visualize how they may come into play in an emergency. These observations are then mapped onto her detailed knowledge of the district. Vulnerable sites have been regularly inspected. Contingency plans have been envisioned. Rescue routes, roadblocks, traffic patterns, prior incidents, and a multitude of human and geographic factors have been assessed and monitored. Meanwhile, at the fire station, vehicles and equipment have been checked, and supplies used in prior missions replenished. When the commander arrives and takes control, she and her team are prepared to act.

When emergency incidents occur, the dispatchers—firefighters who field initial calls—are a crucial link between intelligence gathering and effective action. Their ability to obtain, interpret and clearly convey the relevant information—from the big picture to the smallest details—is indispensable. This knowledge becomes the basis for a dispatcher's consequential act of judgment: determining the type of emergency that is taking place. As the appropriate human resources, vehicles and equipment are quickly mobilized, the dispatcher describes the emergency incident to the team members who are already on the way. This primes the firefighters about what to expect, so they can start thinking about plans and contingencies before arriving at the scene. As a Chicago Fire Department veteran commander remarked to us, "When you hear the voice of certain dispatchers on the radio, your confidence and readiness skyrocket. You know that everything they tell you has been carefully considered and based on experience. They are fully invested in the success and safety of the team. They've got your back."

Calculus of Goals and Risks

Firefighters are mission-driven public servants whose actions are governed by three overarching objectives. They, in order of importance, are: 1) life safety,

2) incident stabilization, and, 3) property conservation. Accompanying this clear Commander's Intent is a guiding principle: the well-being of citizens comes before that of the firefighters. Firefighters routinely act on this mandate, putting their own lives at risk when the safety of others is concerned.

Every emergency incident involves a series of decisions regarding the amount of risk that is required to achieve these objectives. A significant amount of risk may be taken to stabilize the situation if an escalation may endanger civilian lives. In contrast, property conservation would not usually involve a high level of risk-taking. This strategic calculus, grounded in risk intelligence, helps balance goals, risk and available resources. Ingraining this risk-centric way of thinking into practices and cultures (albeit not necessarily in these terms) is one of the top priorities of the fire service leaders, notes Eric Tade, Chief of the Denver Fire Department.

Positioned for Action

Recall that it is the dispatcher who makes the first pivotal judgment: determining the type of emergency at hand or, in Clausewitz's words, the "nature of the war" on which the firefighters are about to embark. He then uses a predefined "run matrix" to activate the necessary resources and personnel. In fact, different types of emergencies—think of terrorist attacks vs. plane crashes or chemical spills—necessitate different numbers of firefighters, quantities and types of vehicles, and supplies. For example, a routine traffic accident may warrant the deployment of one fire engine, one fire truck and a district chief. In contrast, a fire at a high-rise may require many multiples of those resources as well as the elite "special forces" of the fire service trained in forcible entry, hazardous materials and buildings on the verge of collapse. These predefined protocols—according to which the initial resources necessary for various types of emergencies have been rigorously analyzed and institutionalized—are an important contributor to the firefighters' bias for action.

The dispatcher hands over the mantle of risk intelligence and decision-making to the first fire officer who arrives at the scene. Upon announcing command, the officer's responsibility is to further evaluate the situation, determine if additional resources are needed, create the initial plan of attack and further prime those en route about the incident. Depending on the reality on the ground, the initial attack plan can be offensive, defensive or transitional (defensive that may morph info offensive if circumstances allow). Command is transferred to the more senior officers as they arrive and eventually to the stationary incident commander. The situation is continually reassessed, with the attack plan reconfirmed or readjusted.

Major emergency incidents—such as natural disasters, terrorist attacks or large fires—may involve hundreds of firefighters, massive amounts of equipment, complex logistics and operations spanning days, weeks or months. Effectively responding to such incidents necessitates the creation of entirely new *ad-hoc organizations* in real time. These organizations may involve very elaborate, multi-layered hierarchies of what Chuck's long-time colleague General Stanley McChrystal calls "teams of teams." Companies are very quickly assigned a clearly defined functional role[116] and a geographical area. Shared understanding of the environment—that is obtained through multifaceted risk intelligence that flows top-down and bottom-up—is effectively communicated via formal protocols. Decisions up and down the command chain are grounded in the strategic calculus of goals, risks and resources. Calculated decisions are preferred to inaction.

In order to ensure orderly communication and controlled execution, fire service commanders are trained to be highly cognizant of what constitutes an appropriate span of control: the number of teams they directly oversee during an emergency incident. If this number exceeds a certain threshold (e.g., five for a fast-moving event) as additional resources are brought in, a new organizational level is created. This practice fosters an orderly flow of information up and down the command chain. Thus, the incident commander will communicate with only section chiefs who, in turn, will communicate with only the incident commander and the branch directors. Division and group supervisors will communicate only with their superiors. There is, however, an important exception: everyone is allowed—and expected—to notify the Incident Commander and other team members if something extremely consequential is detected. In the fire service, fighting for risk intelligence is everyone's responsibility.

The firefighters' capacity to build and evolve elaborate organizations in real time and under pressure is enabled by a command-and-control philosophy akin to Mission Command and codified in the National Incident Management System (NIMS). NIMS specifies broad parameters and standards—operational guidance and the boundaries of initiative—so that ad hoc organizations can be both robust and custom-tailored to the unique circumstances of the emergency incident.[117] As a result, centralized planning and direction are seamlessly melded with empowered decentralized execution, positioning firefighters for decisive and effective action even in the most uncertain and quickly changing environments, like the Glendale fire.

The culture of courage, excellence, dependability and selflessness binds this all together. Indeed, when speaking with firefighters of all ranks, it is striking to observe that these qualities are viewed as routine and expected. They have been deeply ingrained in the identity and culture of the firefighters for generations, engendering trust and creating a setting conducive to agility. As Chief Edward Croker of the New York Fire Department famously observed over a century ago, "When a man becomes a fireman, his greatest act of bravery has been accomplished. What he does after that is all in the line of work."[118]

~

Agility requires a well-crafted operational philosophy, a clearly articulated Commander's Intent and judiciously set parameters of authority. Yet none of these capabilities and tools will be effective unless they are practiced within a specific organizational environment. In the next chapter, we'll examine specific leadership and cultural qualities that create the Agility Setting and foster decisiveness, the second pillar of agility.

CHAPTER 9

DECISIVENESS

"The war in Vietnam was not lost in the field, nor was it lost on the front pages of the New York Times or the college campuses," writes H. R. Mc-Master in *Dereliction of Duty*. It was "lost in Washington, DC, even before Americans…realized the country was at war; indeed, even before the first American units were deployed."[119]

When Clausewitz wrote that war is "the continuation of politics by other means," he was inferring that clarity of political objectives is a prerequisite of a successful military campaign. The Vietnam War, described by McMaster as "the war without direction," exemplifies a lack of that clarity. Historians have documented nearly two dozen official justifications for American involvement in Vietnam, ranging from resisting Communist aggression to fighting counter-insurgency and maintaining the integrity of American commitments. Exacerbating the problem were, as historian Harry Summers writes, the "neglect of military strategy in the post-World War II nuclear era," insular decision-making by the White House and the failure of the top military commanders to voice dissent.[120] As a result, in McMaster's words, "Men fought and died without a clear idea of how their actions and sacrifices were contributing to an end of the conflict." In contrast, the North

Vietnamese had totally clear and compelling objectives—defending their homeland and conquering South Vietnam.

The lack of clarity carried over into the absence of a well-defined overarching Commander's Intent. Major decisions were outsourced to the commanders of large units. They generally did what they knew best: deployed excessive firepower to advance near-term objectives, often in reactive ways. The results were usually tactically successful but strategically irrelevant. The US won the vast majority of individual battles, but they did not amount to a coherent campaign, and, hence, never resulted in identifiable and acceptable results. The Vietnam War is a cautionary tale of what happens when decentralized execution is unwittingly used to fill a strategic void, which is a failure of what we call *senior leader business*.

Senior Leader Business

Senior leaders set the course for their organizations, catalyze execution and shape a moral system of values and beliefs. They lead by formal authority and soft power, molding internal cultures and external identities of their organizations. Because these top-brain functions are critical to agility, senior leaders must focus on the decisions and activities that only they can and should do. When they do not, decisions that belong exclusively in the realm of senior leadership become outsourced to organizational silos that are not qualified to make them. Cultures emerge by themselves, with competing values and agendas undermining cohesion and trust, while micromanagement in areas the executives *are* focusing on impairs engagement and initiative.

Developing and owning Commander's Intent is primary to senior leader business. Only senior leaders can design multiple lines of operations synchronized to achieve the overarching objectives and guide the execution of decentralized tactical activities accordingly. Only they can determine the organizational competencies required, set the appropriate level of decentralization and assign the boundaries of initiative—all while anticipating the next mission and reflecting a sense of "what ifs" and "what's next" in their actions and guidance. The formation of effective and cohesive teams, well-tailored to the goals and circumstances at hand, is an important part of their mandate as well. It is they who must quickly ascertain how much trust and empowerment to place in individuals and teams based on the assessment of their dependability, competence and will to win.

Only senior leaders can define and clearly articulate the business the organization is in, continuously reassess it and make adjustments—realigning the firm's operations in some cases and leading the organization into new terrain in others. As de facto Chief Risk Officers, it is they who spearhead the fight for risk intelligence and continually rebalance the portfolio of risks. Given that pivotal strategic and organizational decisions that have a dominant impact on long-term performance, the manner in which risk-taking and risk management are done at the highest levels shapes the mindset and culture of the entire organization.[121]

With all of this to do, senior leaders often focus so intently on these roles that they less vigorously attend to an equally crucial task—creating and nurturing the Agility Setting that leads to cohesion, decisiveness and effective decentralized execution. One key aspect of this setting, that we'll discuss next, is the organization's True North—its purpose, vision, values and norms of behavior. The other is the culture of honesty, accountability and trust—the topics of the following sections.

It is the essence of senior leader business to think deeply about the organization's values and standards, catalyze the buy-in, carefully assess their acceptance and practice—and exemplify them on a daily basis. None of this can be left to chance, allowed to become stale or outsourced to organizational silos and subcultures, or to outside consultants. The leadership communication is critical here because motivational pep talks that are actually directed at increasing productivity and compliance are immediately detected. If the leaders' behaviors or communications are viewed as inauthentic, this will breed cynicism and decimate trust, motivation and performance. In the words of historian John Rhodehamel, "noble words" must become "flesh."[122]

Few things are more detrimental to the morale and culture than the leaders' failure to live up to the organization's True North they proclaim to embrace. This is precisely what happened at an investment company we knew well. This firm was founded on the premise that complex forces have created persistent market inefficiencies that could be exploited. This was entirely inconsistent with the magnitude and nature of the losses that followed. When analyzing the downfall, we expected to hear complex financial and economic explanations, such as market paradigm shifts or the emergence of disruptive players and products. Instead, it was the failure of leadership that became a dominant theme of our conversations with the board of directors and the employees.[123]

After the supposed market inefficiencies proved fleeting (not a surprise for the students of efficient markets), senior executives failed to adjust and put forth a viable strategic vision. Excessive and unfamiliar risks were taken in pursuit of growth and investment returns. Caution expressed by subordinates was treated as disloyalty and dismissed. Moreover, the priority of senior executives to benefit themselves at the expense of other stakeholders had a profoundly toxic impact on the organization, leading to other destructive behaviors.[124]

Of course, these topics—the primacy of True North and the responsibilities of senior leaders—are not new, having garnered a rich body of work, such as Joseph Nye's *The Powers to Lead* and Bill George's *True North*. Our focus in this chapter is how they contribute to agility—namely, the role of leadership and culture in cultivating the Agility Setting that fosters two essential organizational qualities: purposefulness and decisiveness. In this regard, we have found a set of insights from psychological research deeply instructive and aligned with our experience.

One impressive body of work is that of social psychologist Jonathan Haidt, whose book *The Righteous Mind* examines the evolutionary origins of human morality. Of particular relevance to developing the Agility Setting is his argument that all of we humans have an innate "hunger for meaning," a longing to "transcend self-interest and lose ourselves (temporarily and ecstatically) in something that is larger" and nobler than our personal interests.[125] This desire for a compelling shared cause is believed to have propelled our success as a species. The human ability to express shared intentionality, providing what Haidt calls a "mental representation" of a group task to be achieved, is believed to have constituted an important evolutionary leap. Once the understanding of the task (i.e., Commander's Intent) was shared and accepted, members of the group could develop expectations, accountability and rewards based on everyone's contributions to achieving a common objective. This allowed early humans to "collaborate, divide labor and develop shared norms," giving them an enormous competitive advantage in the struggle for survival. Being part of a group that is doing meaningful work activates people's engagement, collaborative spirit and loyalty.

The organization's True North can be formalized and articulated using the OSV process. In addition to universal values, such as integrity, accountability and reliability, it can include standards especially important to agility, such as principled pursuit of truth; fighting for risk intelligence; well-calculated risk-taking; and nurturing the next generation of leaders. They all can be impressed on the whole organization as inviolable mandates, guides to behavior and the road to success—but even more importantly, as social norms.

Framing True North in this way activates a powerful mechanism used by all humans to tailor behaviors to a given situation—the *logic of appropriateness* described by organizational theorist James March. March argues that we all tend to decide how to behave based on our answers to three fundamental questions: "What kind of a situation is this?" "What kind of a person am I?" and "What does a person such as I do in a situation such as this?" The answers to these questions are based on a mutual understanding of "what is true, reasonable, natural, right and good."[126]

The US armed forces persuasively illustrate the power of True North, especially when it's positioned as an obligation of character. As General John Schofield famously observed in 1879, making soldiers of a free country disciplined in battle cannot be achieved through formal authority alone.[127] Instilling the values of duty, honor and country is mission-critical to success. Over time, these shared values—even if unfamiliar and lacking practical meaning for new recruits—become embraced by soldiers from all walks of life, from privates to generals. They are supplemented by the Soldier's Creed: putting the mission first, never quitting and never leaving a fallen comrade behind.

Throughout his career, Chuck has defined respect, mentoring and sharing of risk and outcomes as essential elements of True North for the forces under his command. He has relentlessly emphasized that young men and women performing difficult tasks—unthinkable to the ordinary citizens, in lonely places, under trying circumstances, at an uncompromising standard—need to be inspired, supported and respected by their entire chain of command, all the way to the Commander-in-Chief. He witnessed many remarkable outcomes.

A compelling strategic and moral True North activates deeply seated human aspirations and emotions, satisfies the hunger for meaning and instills social norms throughout the organization. It creates *purposefulness* that both empowers strategic initiatives and guides a myriad of decentralized actions. When the boundaries of initiative are clearly defined, empowered and purposeful team members gain confidence to improvise, innovate and take smart risks in pursuit of the shared objectives, even when circumstances change or plans disintegrate at the first contact with reality.

The Forum of Truth

Successfully operating in environments that are filled with uncertainty and ambiguity requires an organizational setting that supports and rewards the principled pursuit of truth. Said differently, achieving agility is not possible when vigorous evidence-based debate is not consistently practiced. That debate must not be isolated to silos or specific decision-making occasions, like executive team and board meetings. The unfettered exchange of ideas must become the pervasive social norm at all times, at all organizational levels and out to the very edges. When this happens, the whole organization becomes what we call a Forum of Truth.

Many business leaders and experts have argued the case for the rigorous pursuit of truth, in various terms. Ray Dalio, the founder of Bridgewater Associates, commends "radical transparency." Yale University professor Jeffrey Sonnenfeld writes that a "culture of open dissent" is essential to long-term success. Amazon requires its leaders to "seek diverse perspectives and work to disconfirm their beliefs." The executive team at Salesforce.com demands "brutally honest" reports that deliver "raw, unadulterated early warning information 24/7."[128]

This way of thinking has powerful historical precedents as well, as great leaders had often surrounded themselves with accomplished and opinionated advisors. This is how George Washington designed his war council and, according to historian Christopher DeMuth, similar approaches were used by Lincoln, Franklin Roosevelt and Regan.[129] We want to offer some reflections on what we have experienced, and divined from research, about the challenges of establishing this rigorous pursuit of truth throughout an organization, the role of senior leaders in it and why it's so vital to agility.

In recent decades, behavioral psychologists eviscerated the once popular argument of classical economic theory that we are rational homo economicus, inclined to optimally use all available information; make fact-based decisions; and readily change beliefs in response to new evidence. Of course, in this brief chapter we could not possibly cover the host of ways in which human decision-making actually deviates from the rationality ideal. To add to the earlier discussion on how human biases can impair situational awareness and strategic calculus, we want to spotlight here a few deep-seated behaviors that can undermine the principled pursuit of truth and outline how they can be mitigated.

One is our proclivity to construct and become wedded to narratives about a situation or problem that we deem plausible, but which are, in reality, quite flawed. In fact, in *Thinking Fast and Slow*, Daniel Kahneman describes rationality itself not as the breed of logical and optimized thinking it has long been characterized as but rather as the human ability and deep-seated need to construct coherent and reasonable narratives, often at the expense of truth. What is particularly detrimental to organizational decision-making and agility is that the greater the specificity of these stories, the higher the chances that an invalid narrative will be accepted as well-founded, even as highly probable. And, as Kahneman cautions, the more confident people are in a story, whether that's concerning a current situation or how the future will unfold, the more leery we should be because "declarations of high confidence mainly tell you that an individual has constructed" a narrative that is coherent, "not necessarily that it is true."[130]

The innate human need to construct plausible stories goes hand in hand with the confirmation bias, which compels us to disregard or explain away the disconfirming evidence. Indeed, so powerful is its grip that new information that should utterly upend a belief not only often fails to do so but actually strengthens the conviction. Experiments measuring brain activity, like those by cognitive neuroscientist Tali Sharot, have shown that our minds react to information that we agree with as "rewarding stimuli" (like food) while reacting to undesirable information as "aversive stimuli" (like electric shocks).[131] We've all seen many disastrous outcomes due to this phenomenon, in business and other domains.

Some years ago, a leading financial firm suffered significant losses in its value investing division. Value investing requires a great deal of conviction—because it focuses on discovering assets that are, in the eyes of the investor, undervalued. So, naturally, if a portfolio manager already likes an asset and then the price of this asset declines, it becomes so much more attractive. In the case of our client, the internal analyses looked comprehensive and persuasive in arguing this exact point on multiple occasions—all while showing a complete disregard for disconfirming evidence. The data supportive of prior views was highlighted, while the importance of new troubling developments was de-emphasized. As asset prices continued to decline, portfolio managers ended up doubling down a number of times, until the losses were so significant that the company had to close out the positions.

During the post-mortem, one senior executive told us that this experience would have been inconceivable when the company was smaller: a significant price drop would have triggered the fight for risk intelligence. A formal and vigorous discussion involving senior executives and external resources would have taken place, with opposing views presented and carefully evaluated. This process disintegrated during the company's explosive growth. Executives became distracted, and boundaries of initiative became blurred: key decisions could be made without a rigorous debate—as long as their supporting arguments were coherent and well-documented.

Fostering the Pursuit of Truth

For an organization to operate as a Forum of Truth, it must legitimize doubt and dissent and prioritize reason over formal authority. The expectation of a free exchange of ideas, patient and respectful deliberation, and mutual learning and discovery must be fully and forcefully articulated, from the top all the way down. This must include the mandate to treat honest mistakes as opportunities for learning and improvement, not vehicles for humiliation or admonishment. The culture has to promote the understanding that "universal truths" and "objective reality" are extremely tricky, idealized concepts. It must also emphasize that because of differing goals, experiences and risk equations, the same information may mean very different things to any of us vis-à-vis our colleagues, adversaries and other players in our competitive ecosystem.[132]

The only way these norms will actually prevail throughout an organization is if they are exemplified by the senior leaders; framed as part of True North; and institutionalized through processes, performance metrics and incentives. The organization's situational awareness and decision-making—and ultimately, agility—will be decimated if senior leaders suppress dissent or treat it as disloyalty, if they punish the messengers of bad news, if they exhibit willful ignorance, or if they use diffusion of responsibility or plausible deniability as excuses for inaction.

In many of the cases we've written about earlier, from the Korean War to the Fukushima Nuclear Disaster and MF Global, warning signals were ignored, and risk equations were misjudged precisely because the disconfirming evidence was either intentionally suppressed or subconsciously dismissed. Similarly, the risk management failures that doomed Challenger and Columbia shuttles did not stem solely from a lack of competence. The NASA culture that discouraged dissent by ostracizing those who voiced concerns and placing the burden of proof squarely on them played an equally significant role.[133] In the wake of the disasters, NASA changed the approach: whenever concerns and warnings emerged, they were taken seriously, and teams were assigned to analyze them and offer recommendations.[134] This change improved risk intelligence, decision-making and organizational cohesion.

Even when organizations declare the primacy of truth and create processes for vetting decisions expressly for the purpose of giving them tough hearings, people often don't voice opinions and counterarguments or ask questions that could lead to important additional investigation. This is only partly due to everyone's familiarity with hierarchical management that punishes dissent in ways both explicit and implicit. Another reason why people often keep their potential input to themselves is their deep-seated concern with what Darwin called "the praise and blame" of their colleagues.[135] This fear of reputational damage is at the core of groupthink, which we have all witnessed—with our colleagues agreeing with a plan or analysis that we could clearly see was invalid, or at least incomplete, and which we suspected most of them could see as such too. That is why it is critical that senior leaders position the pursuit of truth—and everyone's active engagement in it—as both a job requirement and a social norm.

The challenges presented by this complex mix of behavioral biases, leadership practices and organizational cultures are amplified by an additional powerful force that must be preemptively dealt with. Due to what is referred to in psychological research as human context dependency, specific circumstances under which we are exposed to information, the way in which it is presented, and so many other factors of the context in which we are making decisions have a huge effect on both the process of deliberation and the outcome.[136] As the following examples illustrate, the *choice architecture*—ways in which information and possible solutions are presented for discussion—must be carefully evaluated, especially when pivotal strategic and organizational decisions are being made.

When Verizon and Sprint set out to reduce costs a number of years ago, the companies utilized different choice architectures. At Verizon, lines of business were instructed to propose cuts relative to prior years' budgets. In contrast, at Sprint the unit heads were directed to start with a clean sheet and create a budget based on the expected benefits of expenditures and their role in advancing the firm's strategy.[137] In our experience, these alternative approaches usually lead to very different outcomes.

As discussed earlier in the book, complex organizations are commonly exposed to large numbers of individual risks. Unless these risks are properly aggregated, boards and leadership teams end up judging the firm's risk appetite and its alignment with goals and resources based on dozens of disparate line items. As we have witnessed on multiple occasions, very different conclusions may be reached based on the order in which risks are listed and the language in which vulnerabilities, consequences and rare events are described. A previously "unacceptably high" risk profile may be deemed totally acceptable at the next board meeting if risks happen to be rearranged or framed differently—even with the best of intentions.

The organization's ability to function as a Forum of Truth becomes especially important when it operates in environments dominated by powerful (and offer erroneous) popular narratives. As Nobel Prize winning economist Robert Shiller observed, many economic and financial phenomena—such as recessions, asset bubbles or financial crises—can be linked to viral "epidemics of ideas" deliberately used by some people and unwittingly adopted by others.[138] Such narratives that are in his words "mixtures of fact and emotion" based on "varying degrees of truth," can become juggernauts and must be detected and proactively debunked.

In their book *Warnings*, Richard Clarke and R. P. Eddy describe the belief once widely held across the US intelligence community that "no Arab nation has ever gone to war—and thus will never go to war—with another Arab nation." This assumption prevented the US and its Middle Eastern allies from effectively assessing signals that Iraq was about to invade Kuwait in 1990. Similarly, in the buildup to the Great Recession, the dominant narrative that "housing prices across the United States never decline simultaneously" created an over-reliance on geographical diversification as a risk mitigator. This narrative—exploited by some and not questioned by others—permeated a wide range of investment products, corporate practices and credit ratings, setting in motion a lethal vicious cycle.

When a concerted fight for risk intelligence takes place in an environment of trust that prioritizes evidence, deliberation and honesty, organizations become positioned for agility. They examine evidence from multiple perspectives, detect invalid assumptions and potential landmines, and challenge themselves about what they know and don't know. This enables them to gain situational awareness, effectively assess environmental changes and risk equations, and shape productive responses.

One last point we'll make here is that with the deterioration of standards of truth in the culture at large in recent years, the need for organizations to consistently operate as a Forum of Truth is all the more urgent. What may seem to be just basic common sense regarding the ethics of truthfulness in a society has been under assault.[139] The outside culture is sure to permeate organizational bounds, but by prioritizing truth, and a vigorous demonstration of its relentless pursuit in practice, we can beat back the onslaught.

The Agility Setting

On a battlefield—be it warfare, government or business—trust is a non-negotiable requirement for winning and persevering under the most dire of circumstances. It is the binding agent that suppresses selfishness and fosters mutual respect, cooperation and reciprocity. As Darwin famously observed in *The Descent of Man*, "selfish and contentious people will not cohere, and without coherence nothing can be effected."[140] The culture of trust is one of the most important enablers of agility.

We have found that it's helpful to think of trust as an outcome of a series of risk transactions. The first transaction is that of one person entrusting someone else with an asset or task based on a belief in their trustworthiness, competence and dependability. Because the entrusted person values the risk-taker's faith in their abilities and character, they are motivated to follow through on the expectations. The underlying biological mechanism of this process is now well understood. Neuroscientific research has demonstrated that a show of trust causes the entrusted person's brain to experience a surge of oxytocin, the bonding hormone. If the risk-taker's confidence in the entrusted pereson is validated, his or her brain experiences a similar chemical reaction. Hence a virtuous cycle of trust-building is fostered. But it's also vital to appreciate the inherent fragility of trust. Relationships built over many years can be ruined by a single act of deception or betrayal.[141]

A solid foundation of trust is created when empowerment is accompanied by a culture of accountability. Of course, the importance that everyone in an organization must know that they will be held accountable for the outcomes of their actions is well established, with leadership advice often focusing on extrinsic accountability. Each person in an organization is held responsible for tasks or assets. Transparency and controls ensure that results are properly reported and evaluated against expectations. Provided that all of this is based on clear and specific expectations,[142] people receive immediate feedback on whether or not they're meeting them and incentives encourage appropriate behaviors, the accountability is fostered. Motivating people in this fashion has, without doubt, proven effective.

But the intrinsic dimension of accountability is equally, if not more, important. What we find less widely appreciated is that people actually want accountability, it does not have to be brandished over them in threatening ways. Most people have a strong intrinsic drive to be accountable because it's a prerequisite for being respected and accepted by a group, whether that's their team or their circle of friends and family. Our innate desire to belong, therefore, creates a powerful self-driven incentive to be accountable. Seen from this perspective, accountability can be positive and inspirational: it fosters a strong sense of pride in fulfilling our obligations and in taking responsibility for our failures. When the True North, the Forum of Truth and other requirements of agility are positioned as social norms, the reciprocal nature of accountability—between leaders and their subordinates and among the team members—results in all parties feeling a sense of duty in living up to their end of the bargain.

Trust is essential for nearly every aspect of agility. When troubling environmental signals are detected, trust will give our team members the confidence to bear bad news. When the meaning of these often ambiguous signals is debated—or when we are shaping our responses to change and evaluating alternatives—our colleagues will be willing to question assumptions and express dissenting views. In decentralized execution, it is trust that drives smart risk-taking and improvisation as part of bold and purposeful disciplined initiative. That is why, as a central tenet of Mission Command, trust is key to creating a bias for action.

But there is much more to the role of empowerment, accountability and trust in fostering agility. Imagine the following organizational environment. Employees understand that their vigilance is considered indispensable in detecting and assessing environmental changes so that the leaders can use rigorous strategic calculus to align goals and risk. They know that the leadership appreciates their contributions to evidence-based discussions and that thanks to their honesty and contributions, their organizations will be better positioned to uncover hidden vulnerabilities and comprehensively assess the potential positive and negative consequences of risk.

This setting is essential to agility because it results in what Kahneman calls a *special kind of engagement,* and Haidt calls *exploratory thinking.* When people are empowered and engaged in this fashion, writes Kahneman, they become "more alert, more vigilant, more skeptical about their intuitions and less willing to be satisfied with superficially attractive answers."[143] Thus, gut reactions give way to evidence-based judgments, and employees learn to recognize on their own the situations they should investigate and report about. Haidt adds that exploratory thinking results in a greater willingness to revise beliefs in response to evidence. It thrives when people know that they will be held accountable for both the outcomes and the quality of the decision-making process, and when they believe that their colleagues are well-informed and interested in the accuracy of information.[144]

A large body of psychological research has highlighted other benefits germane to agility. Empowered and accountable employees feel in control of their lives, which is one of the strongest human desires. They are more committed to a shared purpose and more capable of thinking abstractly, integrating information and uncovering patterns and relationships in data. They are more willing to take risk and show initiative, more focused on capturing opportunities, not just on mitigating threats.

Special Brand of Leadership

Those who exemplify the special brand of leadership relentlessly attend to senior leader business. They put forth a viable and compelling strategic vision that keeps the organization purposeful and relevant. They inspire confidence, share stakes in risk and outcomes, and decisively act when threats or opportunities arise. They form effective teams and equip them with requisite skills and authority to exercise initiative boldly and creatively. Such leaders define, own, communicate and relentlessly nurture the culture of accountability and trust. They consistently demonstrate that a principled pursuit of truth requires willingness to change beliefs based on new evidence. They devote concerted effort to developing the next generations of leaders. By doing so, they shape the setting that underpins the pillars and the process of agility.

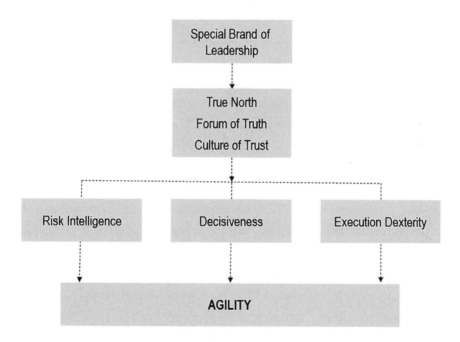

The Agility Setting

The special brand of leadership builds enduring cultures conducive to agility because it powerfully activates the core foundations of morality described in the work of Haidt.[145] When the leaders' actions are aligned with their professed beliefs and goals, their *authority* will be perceived as legitimate, and vice versa. Importantly, this applies not only to individual leaders but also to institutions in a position of power. As a case in point, the authority of the Securities and Exchange Commission was seriously undermined when it disclosed in 2017 that one year earlier, hackers penetrated its electronic system that contains non-public data about corporate earnings and actions, profiting from the inside information. The SEC not only failed to promptly disclose the data breach externally—which is a strict requirement for the companies it regulates—but its employees failed to inform the agency's own commissioners about the breach for many months.[146]

When leaders relentlessly invest in authentic relationships, demonstrate care and empathy for their people, mentor and inspire, they harness the power of other core foundations of morality: *liberty* and *loyalty*. Trust, collaboration and dependability take root throughout the organization when subordinates don't feel exploited or oppressed by a coercive power, when they believe that executives have a genuine concern for their well-being, respect for their contributions and interest in helping them realize full potential.[147] Throughout, the personal qualities of leaders—whether they project sincerity and humility, how they treat people and confront adversity, whether they are willing to sacrifice for a shared cause—play a key role.

When one of our clients faced an existential uncertainty, the company's workforce remained remarkably motivated and engaged. This firm played an important role in the global economy and markets, and this fact unified the organization around an inspirational common purpose. This purposefulness was critical in holding the company together, but so was the relentless commitment by the leaders to invest in their people. The firm couldn't guarantee compensation or even employment over any meaningful time frame, so it created a variety of educational and professional growth programs that made the workforce feel more engaged and fulfilled, as individuals and as professionals. The employees felt that with each passing day, they became more knowledgeable, more experienced and more valuable to future employers. Strong performance and high retention followed.

On the flip side, when executives deliberately undermine trust, refuse to take responsibility, or practice fear-based or transactional management styles, the long-term damage to exploratory thinking, cohesion and agility is profound. In a well-known case in point, F. Ross Johnson, the chief executive of RJR Nabisco vividly portrayed in *Barbarians at the Gate*, used to openly boast how he deliberately withheld information and kept employees off balance by unexpectedly buying and selling businesses and changing organizational structures. In another example, a toxic culture at a well-known international firm proved incompatible with agility. From its inception, the firm's senior executives designed processes and systems that reduced the firm's dependency on specific individuals, with the express intent to make most employees easily replaceable. The firm remained committed to this philosophy through many years of skillful execution and exploitation of market opportunities. By all metrics of financial performance, growth and prominence, this firm has been unequivocally successful. However, the culture of stress and distrust has manifested itself in one important respect: most of the firm's forays into products and services that require original thinking, ingenuity and specialized talents have been largely unsuccessful. To this day, the company "thrives" only in the realm of commoditized activities performed by replaceable and disengaged employees.

A Case Study in Leadership and Culture

In the previous chapter, we took a close look at the agility of leading fire departments in the US, showing that their lasting success goes far beyond quick thinking or inborn reflexes. Firefighters maintain keen situational awareness and make calculated decisions through multifaceted risk intelligence. In emergency incidents, they create a bias for action by constructing, in real time, ad hoc hierarchical organizations where top-down strategy and planning are effectively executed by empowered teams. In this section, we show that leadership, culture and the Forum of Truth play an equally critical role in the preparedness, decisiveness and agility of firefighters.

As one may expect, the effectiveness of firefights rests on a great deal of formal education and training. However, graduating from a fire academy and going through ongoing continuing education is just a start. As a cultural mindset and a standard of excellence, fire crews are expected to train every day, which is rigorously monitored by the fire chiefs. This training involves a study of vulnerabilities across their district as well as development of pre-plans for at-risk sites. On a regular basis, fire teams train at controlled sites that simulate real-life situations, where skills can be improved, and strategies and contingency plans discussed. Such training and planning—which are akin to military war games—are universally viewed as essential to the craft of firefighting and its mindset of constant improvement. They often pave the way to proactive prevention and protection strategies as well.[148]

Consistent with the best practices across industries and professions, once a real-life emergency or a training session is over, firefighters return to the station to debrief and discuss lessons learned. By all accounts, these "kitchen-table academies" are invaluable not only for constant improvement but also for building relationships and trust. Whether the team is cooking, resting or checking equipment, stories about successful missions, adversity, mistakes, losses and acts of heroism are routine. What's more, the eye is always on the future: how to better react to the unexpected, remain calm in life-and-death situations, instill confidence in yourself and your team, and never leave a firefighter behind.

Of course, fire commanders devote a concerted effort to ensuring that all fire crews are sufficiently skilled and experienced to deal with any emergency incident. Interestingly, this process is balanced with a long-standing practice of some large fire departments to allow firefighters after several years of service to request a transfer to a different fire station. Officers can urge team members to stay or encourage others to join their team, but they cannot order anyone to do so. This practice makes fire departments a rare example of paramilitary organizations in which the rank-and-file get to essentially *select* their leaders.[149] In fact, while many transfer requests are driven by personal circumstances, a significant portion is related to the qualities and reputation of leaders. It is not unusual that the arrival of a competent and inspirational captain spurs a large number of requests to transfer to that command. The opposite is also common: when firefighters do not respect leaders or disagree with their philosophy or style, such organizations are likely to experience challenges in retaining top talent and fostering engagement and cohesion.

The collective identity of firefighters has been shaped and reinforced over many generations. Being a *real* firefighter is believed to exemplify courage, dependability and dedication. It means constantly improving by drawing on the vast experience of those who came before you. It also means diligently following tried-and-tested practices and putting your life on the line. Paradoxically, this commitment to tradition can be a double-edged sword at times, leading to a resistance to change. While the firefighters' commitment to excellence and continual improvement is unwavering, sometimes it stands for "doing things the way they have been successfully done for a long time—only better." Thus, when new scientific discoveries or technological advances create an opportunity to make a leap in effectiveness or safety, fire service leaders often need to overcome resistance by diligently educating and inspiring their subordinates, clearly articulating benefits and engendering a broad buy-in.[150]

~

As a pillar of agility, decisiveness positions organizations to act in a timely and calculated manner when opportunities and challenges arise. It is a powerful remedy against inaction and paralysis induced by uncertainty, the fog of conflict, the fear of failure or distrust. Agility rests not just on a bias for any action, but on a bias for deliberate action that follows a fight for risk intelligence and an evidence-based inquiry and debate.

Deliberate is the opposite of impulsive, hasty or accidental. It implies purposefulness, intentionality and confidence. Deliberate decisions and actions are explicitly designed and sequenced to advance the organization's strategy and priorities. They are an outcome of preparedness and planning. They are executed evenhandedly and systematically when the moment is right. They are based on a carefully considered risk transaction: trusting that the team assigned to carry out a mission is cohesive, motivated, capable and unified around the shared True North. Thus, decisiveness is an outcome of the Agility Setting; a well-understood Commander's Intent; clear boundaries of initiative; and the culture of honesty, empowerment and trust—all created and relentlessly nurtured by the special brand of leadership.

As alluded to earlier, decisiveness is key to both strategic and tactical agility. It enables entire organizations to move with the speed of relevance: detect and assess major trends and environmental changes and dynamically adapt their strategic visions, business models, human capital and campaign plans. Equally important, it also fosters aggressive execution of the strategy, where the local knowledge and proximity to action enable timely decisions and actions. Thus, tactical agility enables empowered teams and employees to move with the speed of the challenge: take smart risks, capture opportunities, improvise and innovate within clearly defined boundaries of initiative. Notice that some of the language we use in describing strategic and tactical agility builds on the work of Stephen M. R. Covey who has argued that for any organization, the speed and the effectiveness of its operations are a function of trust.[151]

Once an agile organization detects and assesses an environmental change, shapes a strategy within the Forum of Truth and is ready for a decisive action, the ultimate effectiveness of execution will rest on its mastery of a rich arsenal of tools and capabilities cultivated in advance. This third pillar of agility, execution dexterity, is discussed next.

CHAPTER 10

EXECUTION DEXTERITY

In describing the United States as the "arsenal of democracy" in his 1940 address to the nation, Franklin D. Roosevelt outlined his vision for the country's initial role in World War II.[152] He warned that American civilization was facing an existential danger. Inaction was not an option, and neither was appeasement of the Axis powers. Defending the US and preserving its way of life meant becoming a "militaristic power on the basis of war economy."

To that end, American "industrial genius," technological superiority, and vast financial and human resources must be deployed, he argued, to convert the makers of farm equipment, automobiles, lawn mowers and sewing machines into the manufacturers of "fuses and bomb packing crates and telescope mounts and shells and pistols and tanks." So effective was the national mobilization that the US was able to expand its industrial capacity, resource a two-ocean Navy, build a massive strategic bombing force and supply the Allies with vital military equipment, weaponry and materials.

Three years later, when direct US military involvement became inevitable, a shrewd strategic calculus of goals and risks shaped General George Marshall's daring "90-division gamble." Marshall made the pivotal decision to limit the US Army's ground combat strength to ninety divisions, rather than two hundred, as was originally considered. He had faith in the fighting qualities of American soldiers, but he had also determined that the larger number of divisions would put the nation's economy at risk, seriously interfere with arming the Allied troops, and constitute an inefficient use of the country's resources and competitive advantages. In the language of this book, Marshall's deployment of the military levers was based on an astute assessment of the country's risk appetite as well as of the strategic value of its non-military levers in fighting the war. Army Chief of Military History Maurice Matloff wrote that "of all the calculated risks taken by General George C. Marshall in World War II, none was bolder."[153]

Both Marshall and Roosevelt understood that the US had a powerful competitive advantage in the business levers it could deploy. The already formidable US industrial sector was repurposed to serve the war effort to such an extent that a third of the country's industrial output became dedicated directly to the war.[154] This was not done by government order or appropriation; it was done through the negotiation of contracts on favorable business terms. As historian Doris Kearns Goodwin has written, "Without the cooperation of industry, massive production would never get off the ground. So the challenge was to bring the proprietors of the nation's chief economic assets into the defense effort as active participants."[155] As part of this effort, Roosevelt harnessed the talents of many of the nation's top business executives for the purposes of government planning and oversight of war production, actually bringing them into the government.

Great ingenuity was also used in deploying financial levers. The Reconstruction Finance Corporation (RFC), established during the Great Depression to provide emergency funds to financial institutions and loans to state and city governments to fund infrastructure projects, was given a wide range of new responsibilities and a massive increase of funding. Among a host of activities, the RFC managed the creation and running of eight corporations to produce materials needed for the war, including the development of synthetic rubber. It funded the construction and expansion of factories and provided subsidies to existing businesses both to support their production of essential materials and to act as price controls. It ran programs for the salvage of scrap metals and made strategic purchases of materials from overseas supplies to keep them out of the hands of the enemy.[156]

The total range of levers deployed and the dexterity with which they were used are highlighted by Goodwin: "The several facets of the wartime economy worked in tandem. The war was financed by a combination of taxes and bonds, but FDR's control of the Federal Reserve guaranteed that interest rates would stay low. Wage and price control and rationing made sure that full employment and shortages did not create inflation or hoarding as a side effect. Public investment provided the capital that the factories needed. A labor-business entente assured the absence of disruptive strikes. It was all of a piece."[157] The execution of the strategy proved such a success that it not only fulfilled America's World War II objectives but also fueled the nation's economic and military superiority for decades to come.

The choices and tradeoffs inherent in the "arsenal of democracy" doctrine remain relevant to this day, upheld in the broadly accepted view of "the business the US is in" as a country, as well as the society's risk appetite. In major military conflicts—where its national interests are believed to be directly at stake—the US remains willing to put American lives at risk. However, when it comes to the conflicts of indirect importance or UN peacekeeping missions, the nation tends to lend its support by supplying arms, engaging in limited military operations and providing financial, training and intelligence assistance. Difficult choices regarding the levers that should be pulled in pursuit of geopolitical and national security objectives come prominently on display when proposals for cutting foreign aid or diverting resources away from the likes of the State Department, USAID or the Peace Corps periodically resurface. In those cases, US military and government leaders have for the most part been steadfast in pointing out that the country can either focus on preventing conflicts by investing in diplomacy, soft power and economic development abroad or it will need to make more ammunition and put men and women in uniform in harm's way.[158]

Levers of Agility

We've said earlier that an organization exhibits execution dexterity when it dynamically and proficiently uses all of the capabilities and tools at its disposal in planning, risk-taking and strategy implementation. To formalize the concept here, we define execution dexterity as:

> *The organizational ability to effectively utilize the full arsenal of levers in executing plans and responding to environmental changes.*

Execution dexterity requires a number of key capabilities. The organization must recognize all levers at its disposal and develop each lever to be of sufficient quality and capacity. It must achieve the mastery of each lever. It must develop the capacity to holistically decide—based on specific circumstances at hand—how levers should be deployed, and in what combinations, to achieve objectives. Through fighting for risk intelligence and planning, the organization must also be able to evaluate the potential future needs and uses of levers, so that it can start developing them in advance.

There are six main classes of levers: government, business, risk, organizational, communication and physical.

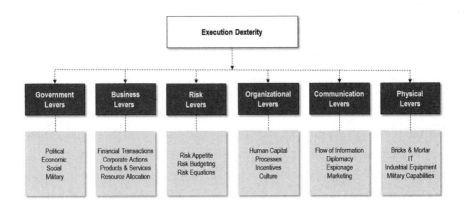

The Levers of Agility

Government levers encompass tools and capabilities that affect political environments, economic and social policies, and warfare. They include fiscal and monetary policies, regulation, economic sanctions, military campaigns and regime changes.

Business levers span the domains of financial transactions (investments, hedging and insurance), corporate actions (mergers and acquisitions, spinoffs and dividends), products and services, and resource allocation (capital, talent and operational bandwidth). Business levers also include research and development, vertical integration, pricing, cross-selling and business model transformations.

Risk levers deal with the active management of the organization's portfolio of risks. They include risk appetite, risk budgeting (allocation of risk across lines of business, initiatives or risk types) and mechanisms for altering risk equations. Execution dexterity requires that these levers are continually used to align our goals, risk and capacity. Far too many organizations fail to utilize a full set of risk levers or to use risk levers explicitly, not as mere side effects of business and organizational decisions. Those who do have a significant competitive advantage.

Organizational levers span processes, cultures, organizational design, incentives and a wide range of tools that deal with human capital, from talent acquisition and training to cultivation of the next generation of leaders. Organizational levers we've introduced in this book include the mechanism for changing the level of decentralization and approaches to cultivating a culture of trust, a Forum of Truth and the special brand of leadership.

Communication levers span the internal flow of information, strategic communications, marketing and branding. In international affairs, national intelligence and military realms, communication levers include diplomacy, propaganda, misinformation campaigns and information collection.

Physical levers include infrastructure and equipment, such as information technology, manufacturing equipment, transportation capabilities and analytical systems.

Achieving complex strategic, financial or operational objectives requires simultaneous use of multiple levers as in the following three examples.

Skillful deployment of risk levers was crucial to the success of Goldman Sachs in withstanding and exploiting the global financial crisis of 2008–09. Because the firm habitually operates in a mover mode, with both top and bottom brains being proactive and engaged, it was able to detect and assess the cracks in the US housing market earlier than its peers. Disconcerting environmental signals were promptly communicated. Based on the detailed information on the firm's portfolio of risks available in real time, the leadership team used strategic calculus to shape a comprehensive plan of action. It was based on a pivotal act of judgment: in anticipation of a broader crisis, reduce the firm's overall risk appetite as well as exposures to specific types of risk.

The deployment of risk levers was implemented through a number of financial strategies. Starting as early as December of 2006, Goldman Sachs sold mortgage loans and securities and purchased insurance against credit losses.[159] As the crisis continued to intensify, a multitude of other business levers were deployed. The size of the balance sheet was shrunk. On the asset side, real estate and illiquid holdings were reduced, and the amount of cash was increased. On the liability side, short-term debt and collateralized liabilities were paired down, while the relative sizes of bank deposits and long-term debt were increased. Goldman also secured a $5 billion investment from Berkshire Hathaway that in addition to reducing risk also served as a communication lever, as it sent a message to the market that significantly improved confidence in the firm's soundness.

In earlier chapters, we described how the culture of empowerment and clearly defined boundaries of initiative can foster independent decision-making and bold initiative across the organization. In terms of execution dexterity, decentralization is an organizational level that goes hand-in-hand with business, communication and risk levers. In fact, trusting subordinates to make independent decisions that are effective, ethical and aligned with Commander's Intent—and being willing to tolerate inevitable mistakes and setbacks—requires an increase in the leaders' risk appetite. Since effective decentralization is only possible when junior commanders are properly educated, trained and developed as leaders, a significant investment of time and resources (the deployment of business levers) is required.

During the fall of 1972, the peace talks between the US and North Vietnam broke down, with diplomacy and public relations (communication levers) proving insufficient. To force the adversaries back to the negotiating table, President Nixon and Henry Kissinger pursued a multifaceted campaign that required an increase in risk appetite. This effort included Operation Linebacker II, a short-duration limited-objective military campaign that aimed to destroy specific, previously untargeted industrial and military complexes and to blockade international ports by mining. The aerial bombardment of the North was conducted with an intensity not seen since World War II. The objectives were accomplished through a carefully planned use of a specific military (physical) lever that offered unique capabilities and competitive advantages—a significant percentage of the US inventory of heavy strategic B-52 bombers. This led to the signing of the Paris Peace Accords that ended the war.

The Need for a Holistic Approach

Until just a few years ago, Wells Fargo enjoyed the enviable status of the world's most valuable financial brand.[160] As a "quintessential" Main Street bank, the company's vision—to "satisfy…customers' financial needs and help them succeed"—was perceived as carefully operationalized and consistently executed. With pride, Wells Fargo has been vocal about its customer-centric business philosophy and distinctive culture. The firm smartly stayed away from some of the risky products and strategies that have plagued Wall Street and some of its commercial banking peers.

Over the years, the bank's ability to use diverse levers to seize opportunities and drive growth and performance has been noteworthy. When Wachovia needed to be rescued following the collapse of Lehman Brothers, Wells Fargo took a disciplined approach amidst a bidding war with Citigroup, making sure that Wachovia's acquisition would advance its business objectives and achieve earnings thresholds.[161] As Wachovia's branches were assimilated and rebranded, Wells Fargo increased its risk appetite, capturing market share in home loans as competitors retreated. The company's opportunism around the Wachovia acquisition followed similarly impressive dynamism in business-as-usual environments. For instance, the firm has long practiced a dynamic asset/liability management process aimed at taking smart interest rate bets and capitalizing on perceived short-term arbitrage opportunities—all subject to rigorously monitored risk limits.

Nonetheless, starting in the early 2000s, the bank came to increasingly rely on one particular business lever—cross-selling of multiple products to customers. The strategy had been touted by the company and external observers alike as one of its most important drivers of success. Already boasting an impressive six products per average customer, Wells Fargo's so-called "Eight is Great" initiative set the goal of expanding this number to eight.[162] As it turned out, while focusing on the business and financial benefits of cross-selling, the bank's senior executives failed to foster a culture consistent with professed values centered on customer success. Pressure to deliver results at all costs was accompanied by the apparent tolerance, and even encouragement, of questionable behaviors. As a result, thousands of employees secretly created millions of unauthorized bank and credit card accounts that generated fees from unaware customers on a staggering scale. Similar grave violations took place in other lines of business, such as wealth management.[163]

Wells Fargo's executives failed to attend to key aspects of senior leader business, some obvious and some more complex. By creating unrealistic performance targets and tolerating behaviors incompatible with the company's stated True North, unethical behaviors were essentially incentivized. But an equally important failure of leadership involved the mismanagement of the firm's portfolio of risks, since pulling the cross-selling lever so aggressively increased the risk of unethical behaviors. This new vulnerability (operational and legal risk), which came along with major financial, reputational and regulatory consequences, should have been proactively mitigated head-on.

Wells Fargo had an opportunity to do this right: to achieve performance objectives through cross-selling, proactive leadership communication regarding the expected norms of behavior and the intolerance for violations of rules could have oriented the entire organization toward True North. Purposeful execution of this strategy within clearly defined boundaries of initiative could have followed, unleashing employee creativity, ingenuity and the full power of tactical agility in pursuit of true value creation for the firm's customers.

The Wells Fargo example illustrates a key point relevant to agility. To ensure that we are positioned for effective action, with as few unanticipated side effects as possible, we need to adopt a holistic approach that can help evaluate: 1) how unexpected interactions among different levers can impair results, 2) how the deployment of levers impacts our portfolio of risks, and 3) whether our use of levers remains consistent with our objectives. Such an approach would have come in handy during the 2011 NATO-led military intervention in Libya intended to bring about a ceasefire in the country's civil war. The original goal was to protect civilians, but it morphed to include regime change. The air bombing campaign—the primary lever deployed in the process—proved inadequate with respect to the broadened objective, contributing to Libya's political and economic collapse and the growth of the Islamic State. The result could have been expected: air campaigns conducted without the support of other military, political and economic levers can only be effective in achieving very specific, limited objectives.

By contrast to the 2011 Libyan bombing campaign, a well calculated airstrike on the country was conducted by the US in 1986, illustrating how several elements of power, including the military, can be used to attain limited political objectives without risking unacceptable consequences. After a series of confrontations with Libyan leader Gaddafi, US forces had prepared and rehearsed a number of contingency operations to address his illegal territorial claims in the Gulf of Sidra, his support for international terrorist groups and his purported desire to develop nuclear weapons. All of these represented a threat to regional and alliance security in Europe and North Africa, and primarily diplomatic and informational tools had been used in attempts to dissuade and deter his activities.

In the spring of 1986, Libya was directly tied to the bombing of a discotheque in West Berlin that killed several and wounded hundreds including US servicemen. Based on previous contingency planning, Operation El Dorado Canyon was designed to conduct a limited air strike on mainland Libya to clearly convey that the country's aggression, especially when directed at US forces and interests, would not be tolerated. The forces were trained, ready and available. A clear understanding of Libyan defenses indicated a limited risk to the strike force. Sufficient alliance support and a clear distancing of the USSR from Libya indicated acceptable diplomatic risk. The objectives were attainable and the risks acceptable—as compared to the unacceptable threats Gaddafi posed to US interests and his overall hostile trajectory.

The strike was a success. While a single US FB-111 Bomber was lost, the message was received. Gaddafi never again targeted specific US interests; greatly diminished his support to terrorist activities and negotiated reparation payments to the victim's families; and by the turn of the century had dismantled his weapons programs. The risk of the strike and its combination of diplomatic, informational and military levers proved to be a well calculated step on the path to putting Gaddafi in a secure box…for a time.

Punching above Weight

In Chapter 1, we paved the way to the concept of execution dexterity by noting that to win through agility, we don't need to be the biggest, the fastest or the strongest. But we must be big enough, strong enough and fast enough—and must develop a capacity to rigorously assess a situation and decide how, when and to what end the appropriate combinations of levers should be deployed. That way, we can effectively compete with, or even prevail over, competitors with far superior capabilities.

Take the case of Israel. Surrounded by adversaries, it cannot afford to rely only on conventional means of defense, so the country's operating philosophy is to utilize a vast arsenal of levers to change critical risk equations in its favor. It maintains military and technological edge through significant ongoing investments: with about 4.5 percent of the country's GDP devoted to R&D, Israel has one of the world's most entrepreneurial and innovative economies.[164] It uses arms diplomacy to expand spheres of influence and generate revenues. Through world-leading innovation in water desalination and desert irrigation, Israel has achieved strong food and water security—while becoming a major supplier of produce to Europe.

In military conflicts, Israel uses hybrid warfare, where powerful combinations of conventional forces, intelligence, special forces, and electronic and cyberwarfare are simultaneously deployed. Equally important, Israel uses deterrence—stemming from the alleged possession of nuclear weapons, technological superiority, a strong relationship with the United States and a long track record of decisive responses to provocations—to decrease the likelihood of adversarial actions.

One of the main themes of our book is that the need for agility arises from the presence of uncertainty and adversaries. If we yield the initiative, if we tolerate strategic contradictions, if we don't creatively use the levers at our disposal—and arm ourselves with new capabilities that are emerging—we are likely to find ourselves outmaneuvered. One of the most troubling recent examples of this is Russia's deployment of a wide range of levers in pursuit of its global aspirations. Agility is unfortunately not reserved solely for actors with the best of intentions.

Putin's Arsenal of Anti-Democracy

Since the beginning of the twenty-first century, the Russian government under Vladimir Putin has pursued a doctrine aimed at undermining trust in Western democratic systems, destabilizing the post-Cold War international order and restoring Russia's power on the global stage. This has included, as a center of gravity, concerted attempts to strategically handicap the US, drive a wedge between the US and its NATO allies, and affect the outcome of democratic elections. Russia's situational awareness, strategy formulation and execution dexterity contain valuable lessons for Western governments, armed forces and corporate leaders about this era of persistent conflict.

Under Vladimir Putin's leadership, Russia has been very astute at detecting pivotal environmental changes. In the wake of the 9/11 terrorist attacks, the US wars in Afghanistan and Iraq not only consumed much of the US military's attention and resources but created tensions between the US and its allies. This was later followed by a lack of a coherent foreign policy; a decline of American leadership in international affairs; and a decrease in appetite for additional military confrontations. These developments presented Russia with an opportunity to shape a bold strategy and deploy a rich and innovative arsenal of levers. The use of these capabilities and tactics has been masterfully tailored to the circumstances at hand.[165]

POLITICAL LEVERS	• Military campaigns (annexation of Crimea, wars in Georgia & Syria) • Attempts at regime change (Montenegro) • Political assassinations (domestically and abroad) • Cyberwarfare (alleged election interference in the US, France, Estonia, and Ukraine; espionage; and counterintelligence)
BUSINESS LEVERS	• Reallocation of economic and human resources to the development of advanced military capabilities as well as to military campaigns • Financial support of populist movements • Arms sales and economic support (Iran, Syria, Egypt and Turkey)
RISK LEVERS	• Increase in risk appetite (slower economic growth due to sanctions, combat casualties, a decline in the oil and gas market share)
ORGANIZATIONAL LEVERS	• Centralization of power • Reorganization and professionalization of the armed forces • Unification of the Russian population around a nationalist purpose
COMMUNICATION LEVERS	• Information warfare directed at fueling social, political, ethnic, and religious tensions (US, Syria, Iraq) • Diplomacy (Iran nuclear deal, North Korea, Syria, UN Security Council obstructionism) • Propaganda at home and abroad
PHYSICAL LEVERS	• Development of advanced military capabilities and tools for projecting military and economic power around the world

Some of Russia's strategies and approaches have been particularly noteworthy. In complementing conventional military, financial and diplomatic tools, it has innovated in information warfare—a composite communication lever that encompasses messaging, propaganda and sophisticated misinformation campaigns. The use of this lever was empowered by physical, business and organizational levers, such as information technology, financial investments and the development of relevant human resources. When we discussed the role of information warfare and cyberattacks in Russia's strategy with General Michael Hayden, the former Director of the Central Intelligence Agency and the National Security Agency, he observed that in and of itself, much of the Russian acquisition of intelligence constitutes standard espionage practice. It is the sustained campaign to *weaponize* this information and systematically deploy it through both traditional and social media channels that has been new.[166]

Recognizing the superiority of US conventional forces, control of the skies and advanced surveillance, Russia has opted to exploit the political and military weaknesses of the US by leveraging risk intelligence, cutting edge technologies, soft power and execution dexterity. The country's innovative use of hybrid warfare was on display during its military campaigns in Syria and Ukraine, where, as described by journalists Nathan Hodge and Julian Barnes, "advanced jamming techniques, electronic surveillance and drones continually improved" the capabilities of the armed forces, making them "more precise and lethal."[167] Russia has also enhanced its conventional military capabilities significantly. In his 2016 testimony on Russia before Senate Armed Services Committee, Lt. General H. R. McMaster observed that while the US Army was engaged in Afghanistan and Iraq, Russia studied US capabilities and vulnerabilities and embarked on an ambitious and largely successful modernization effort. In subsequent conflicts, Russia's combination of unmanned aerial systems, offensive cyber capabilities and advanced electronic warfare showed a high degree of technological sophistication and novel military strategies. Russia continues actively refining and expanding its use of integrated military and nonmilitary capabilities in its quest for greater geopolitical influence.

Strategic initiatives of this magnitude require a comprehensive and clearly articulated strategy. They entail a deliberate and patient reallocation of resources as well as a significant increase in risk appetite, both in terms of upfront investments and willingness to deal with often unpredictable repercussions, such as loss of life and military equipment or international sanctions that stunt economic growth. Equally important, these initiatives require extensive planning and preparedness.

Many of Russia's actions under Vladimir Putin have revealed a unifying theme: they aimed to actively exploit opportunities presented by vulnerabilities, indecisiveness, the lack of cohesion and the absence of a cogent strategy on the part of its adversaries. By seizing the initiative and maintaining a persistent bias for offense, Russia has been able to keep Western democracies largely off balance and on the defensive.

The Chinese general and military theorist Sun Tzu believed that "supreme excellence consists in breaking the enemy's resistance without fighting." Following in Tzu's footsteps, General Valery Gerasimov, the principal architect of the Russian hybrid warfare strategy, has reportedly stated that the goal of the "indirect and asymmetric" warfare his country is continually mastering is to deprive "the opposing side of de facto sovereignty without seizing any territory."[168]

~

In our next and final chapter, we will bring many of the book's themes together—by illustrating the Agility Process, the pillars of agility and the Agility Setting using a fascinating recent business example and a timeless military case study that changed the course of history.

CHAPTER 11

PLANNING FOR AGILITY

At the intersection of technology and finance, many disruptive cycles of innovation have taken place over the past one and a half centuries. Throughout, very few companies have embraced change and continually evolved as deftly as the New York and Mississippi Valley Printing Telegraph Company, better known today as Western Union.

At the company's founding in 1851, the leadership set out to make it a dominant player in the emerging telegraph marketplace.[169] By capitalizing on the opportunities presented by a nascent industry and undeveloped markets, the firm aggressively acquired smaller players and expanded services across the US, Europe and Asia. Rapidly gaining market share and prominence, Western Union (WU) was listed on the New York Stock Exchange in 1865, becoming one of the original eleven stocks in the first Dow Jones Transportation Average index in 1884.

In the ensuing decades, WU continued to decisively respond to change, adroitly adapting its services and business model to the evolution of financial markets and the advent of telephone, fax and the Internet. The company often went on the offense in innovation, such as by leveraging its extensive telegraph network to introduce a money transfer service in 1871, pioneering the first consumer charge card in 1914 and launching the first US domestic communications satellite in 1974. By the turn of the twenty-first century, WU was a Fortune 500 company with operations in over 200 countries and more retail agent locations than McDonald's and Starbucks combined. The firm also had one of the world's most recognizable brands in the realm of cross-currency, cross-border money movement. It was especially known for serving immigrant populations, small and medium-sized businesses, financial institutions and educational organizations.

By deeply thinking about its operating environment throughout the 2000s, WU observed a profound sea change: the emergence of new digital marketplaces, communities and ecosystems. The advent of e-commerce and digital financial services posed an existential threat to the company's relevance, market position and business model, which were centered on physical infrastructure. Given the magnitude of the threat, many industry observers voiced concerns about the company's prospects. Despite a very long track record of successful adaptations, the company faced, in the words of CEO Hikmet Ersek, "a world of doubters wondering if WU would survive." The firm's ability to maintain and expand a leadership position seemed out of the question. The verdict was in: 165-year-old companies are incapable of change.

By the end of the decade, WU's senior leadership made a pivotal strategic decision: transform the firm into a significant player in the new digital marketplace. Needless to say, this was a massive endeavor that involved redefining its value proposition to different groups of stakeholders, fundamentally reevaluating how it viewed and used technology, acquiring new capabilities, and then shaping and executing a coherent campaign plan. The company's lack of required expertise and brand recognition in the digital realm had to be boldly addressed.

In 2011, after a careful evaluation of the competitive landscape involving a fight for risk intelligence and rigorous assessment of its existing businesses, WU's leadership put forth a comprehensive digital transformation plan. This customer-centric, multi-pronged strategy was designed to develop best-in-class digital capabilities and significant online presence—while also boosting the value proposition and efficiency of the traditional brick-and-mortar businesses.

Determining the extent to which the new digital expertise and services should empower the company's traditional lines of business was an important aspect of the strategy development process. An additional fight for risk intelligence was needed to understand the preferences and requirements of the firm's distinctive and loyal customer base. How would these customers respond to a digital offering? What was the importance of physical locations and cash transfers to the different segments of the customer base? Were digital businesses fundamentally different (so should be operated separately) from traditional business lines? In the attempt to answer these questions, the leadership faced deeply ingrained views and assumptions, both internally and externally. As one senior executive commented to us, sharply questioning conventional wisdom and myth-busting were indispensable to the endeavor. It was a Forum of Truth in action.

In the end, the importance of physical locations and cash transactions for certain segments of the customer base was clearly confirmed. But it was also discovered that many current customers would welcome the convenience of registering and performing certain transactions on reliable and customer-friendly digital platforms. A close integration of digital and traditional services was chosen.

Guiding the company through such a sweeping transformation required clear Commander's Intent and strong leadership. The goal entailed not only entering a new business but changing the firm's identity and culture. Pushback was to be expected. New talent would have to be brought in, which posed a risk of creating anxiety and culture shock so had to be managed carefully. Dedicated leaders and teams were critical in making a compelling and inspirational case for change. Delivering early successes was also important, making people across the firm feel excited to be a part of something new and impactful.

WU decisively utilized a rich arsenal of levers to execute the plan. The business levers employed included significant investments in new digital and risk management capabilities, reallocation of resources, new business partnerships and new products.[170] Going on the offense, WU's executives decided to aggressively build on one area of strength: risk management. The company had world-class expertise in managing the risks inherent in cross-border money transfers as well as top-quality compliance and anti-money laundering capabilities. The decision was made to broaden and enhance these strengths, turning its already strong position into a major competitive advantage and a steep barrier to entry in those services for rivals. Some of the advanced capabilities developed by WU included custom algorithms designed to detect and stop, in real time, potentially illicit activities; programs that screened transactions against dozens of US and international sanctions lists and databases; capabilities to place high-risk transfers on hold while verifications were taking place; and fraud hotlines in more than 95 countries and territories. In the process, the firm dramatically increased overall risk management and compliance funding, to approximately $200 million per year.[171] More than 20 percent of the company's workforce became dedicated to compliance functions, and additional human capital encompassing senior law enforcement officials, former regulators and leading banking experts was brought in.

Risk levers were also well deployed. The magnitude of organizational change that was planned required a significant increase in the firm's overall risk appetite. Willingness to make large investments, tolerance for potential mistakes and comfort with uncertainty about the reception of new products and services were critical. The risk that potential disapproval by some stakeholders and financial markets could lead to stock price volatility and temporary underperformance had to be contended with as well.

Extensive use of organizational levers allowed the company to develop the new capabilities and skills while also tapping into a wealth of internal experience. Teams to lead the change were formed, comprised of both WU executives with strong internal reputations and newcomers with deep expertise in digital finance. A concerted effort was made to, in the words of one senior executive, "accelerate the company's metabolism" by fostering a culture of risk-taking and experimentation, with innovations originated and pressure tested in short development cycles.

Communication levers employed included proactive investor relations, marketing and branding. Deployment of physical levers was also noteworthy. In order to gain access to the fintech talent pool in Silicon Valley, the Colorado-based firm decided to house its new digital business in San Francisco, while the company's iconic network of 550,000 retail agent locations around the world was equipped with new technology.

The results were impressive. By 2016, more than 100,000 businesses, including major financial firms, educational institutions, NGOs and small-to-medium-sized businesses relied on WU to make cross-border payments. The firm's main website, WU.com, came to host over 17 million monthly visitors across forty countries, growing revenues at 25 percent per year. The WU app was recognized among "Top 20" apps in finance and downloaded over 3 million times.[172] At the time of this book's writing, the company boasts one of the largest physical and digital platforms, providing a wide range of financial transactions, with operations across more than 200 countries and 130 currencies. Thanks to its strong new technology backbone, WU can move money with extraordinary speed and scale, processing 32 transactions every second and annually completing over 500 million business payments, moving $150 billion per year. The firm's expertise in risk management and compliance has been successfully marketed as an important part of its value proposition, strategic differentiation and competitive advantage.

For over 165 years, WU has embraced disruption and change—and it will need to remain vigilant and agile as the digital and e-commerce revolution carries on in full stride. WU's leadership knows full well that the technology and the operating environment around financial payment systems will continue to rapidly evolve. New disruptive technologies will surely emerge, new market entrants will seek to grab market shares, cybersecurity threats will intensify and regulatory regimes will evolve. All of this will continually threaten business models and competitive advantages, necessitating a relentless fight for risk intelligence and course readjustments carefully shaped and decisively executed within a culture of trust.

Planning for Agility

As we studied a wide range of examples of organizations applying the components of agility with varying degrees of success, Western Union's digital transformation in the face of potential extinction stood out. It comprehensively illustrated the "detect, assess and respond" Agility Process, the pillars of agility and the Agility Setting.

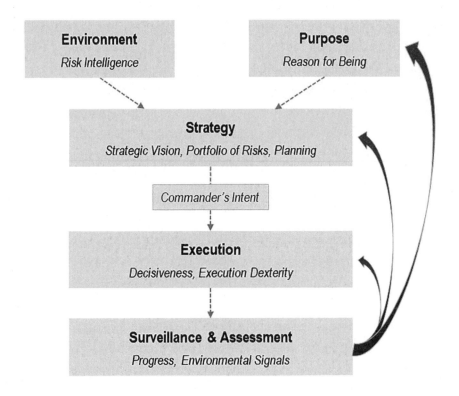

The Agility Process

Of course, the Agility Process is an ongoing and iterative endeavor. The progress of strategy execution and changes in the operating landscape, including those created by our own actions, must be constantly monitored and assessed. The resulting feedback loops and continuous readjustments play a critical role in creating agility. On a tactical level, execution, surveillance and assessment go hand in hand, enriching and empowering one another and leading to continuing refinement of execution strategies. Sometimes, new developments warrant a reassessment of strategic objectives and tolerance for risk. When environmental changes are especially profound, senior leaders may need to step back and holistically tackle the existential questions dealing with the very purpose of the company and the nature of its business. Throughout, the fight for risk intelligence and the way information is presented to decision makers are continuously enhanced. Analytical tools and performance metrics are adjusted to reflect our progress, new developments and our sense of whether we are achieving Commander's Intent and measuring the right things in the right way.

Successfully achieving this in practice requires making agility an integral part of the planning process. This may sound like a contradiction, since most leaders would readily attest that a carefully crafted and detailed plan may, in fact, inhibit agility, even when it is executed skillfully. In the realm of warfare, the German Schlieffen Plan employed during the World War I serves as an instructive example. Years in the making, brilliant in its offensive conception and exquisite in detail, in the end, it ended up being a straitjacket that robbed a very capable German Army of the agility required to meet the unforeseen firepower advantage the twentieth century gave to the defense. Across domains, plans can indeed stifle the whole process, from strategic visualization to tactical execution. In business, examples abound, such as Sony's Betamax VCR debacle. Many are well documented in Michael Raynor's *The Strategy Paradox* and other business literature.

General Dwight Eisenhower famously observed that "plans are worthless, but planning is everything." It is not the existence of formal plans, but the *act* and the *method* of planning that enable agility. The importance of planning lies not in fashioning a sure path to success, but in setting a clear direction, analyzing a wide range of potential scenarios and routes to the goal, and empowering the organization with the necessary intelligence, execution capabilities and boundaries of initiative to monitor, assess and make adjustments as the plan is developed and put in action.

This is the approach developed by the US military in which planning is considered an indispensable competence of senior leaders. Commanders are taught to balance the goals of an operation with a rigorous assessment of the enemy's capabilities and intentions; risks, resources and capacity of the organization—all while seeking to uncover the possible factors that may come into play. As the planning process moves forward, a deeper understanding of the overarching purpose of the mission is formulated. Ongoing surveillance and assessment lead to continuing refinement of execution strategies. The available levers and those that must be developed are also assessed.

Once armed with the commander's goals, priorities and operational guidance, planners develop various potential courses of action. These alternatives are war-gamed in a variety of scenarios to account for differing environmental factors and adversaries with varying capabilities and objectives, often within the so-called action-reaction-counteraction approach. The process concludes with a decision by the commander on the course the organization should take.

The outcome of the planning process is twofold. First is the campaign plan—the senior leaders' view on the best way to reach stated objectives in a given environment and moment in time. This plan enables the entire organization to visualize the unfolding of the whole endeavor—from individual missions on the lowest level to complex operations with multiple lines of action over multiple stages, with careful consideration of their timing. This is imperative if separate lines of operation are to seamlessly come together.

The second outcome is a set of contingency plans developed in light of the uncertainty of future conditions and the unfolding of the plan itself. Contingency plans describe a wide range of "what ifs" and "what's next" spanning both potential challenges and opportunities. They outline alternative paths to realizing the objectives and their required levels of risk. They also provide assessments of how the plan may need to be adjusted or transformed altogether if the operating landscape shifts in certain ways. All of this can be effectively integrated with detection and assessment processes.

Rather than creating formal plans that lie inert between the bindings of thick strategic documents, this approach makes the whole Agility Process come alive. It turns plans into guides, rather than precise "how to" checklists that stifle initiative and agility, allowing us to adroitly shape and manage responses to environmental changes, including major organizational transformations. Other crucial outcomes include situational awareness, exploratory thinking and exchange of ideas that lead to the continual refinement of Commander's Intent. Since this process represents a significant allocation of time and resources at many levels of the organization, the full buy-in of relevant leaders must be assured. This requires that the nature and purpose of the process are clearly and persuasively explained to all involved.

Perhaps no more convincing case could be made than by examining the Allied planning and execution that led to the extraordinary agility prior and during the invasion of Normandy during World War II. It exhibits all components of the Agility Process and Setting being applied in one of the most complex operations ever undertaken, in a situation of intense fog and friction, and with a great deal at stake—the future of freedom as we know it in the Western democracies.

The Battle of Normandy

Operation Overlord, also known as the Battle of Normandy, not only marked a turning point in World War II, it was one of the most pivotal moments in human history. Through critical acts of judgment and comprehensive planning in the preceding years—and then by overcoming significant casualties and setbacks through perseverance and agility in real time—the Allied forces helped shape the post-war international regime and spheres of influence. If the invasion had ended in defeat, the Soviet Union might have become the sole World War II victor, and the world we live in today could have been radically different.

The battle commenced on June 6, 1944, with the air and amphibious assault to gain a foothold on the beaches of Normandy, which was followed by the advance of over two million Allied troops across France, and ended shortly after the liberation of Paris, when the German forces retreated across the Seine on August 30, 1944. The planning of the operation itself—and a myriad of transformational initiatives that came prior—was of extraordinary scope and detail. A crystal-clear purpose was accompanied by the empowerment of disciplined initiative at all levels, out to the very edges of the organizations involved, which led to both strategic and tactical agility.

Strategic Agility

The Battle of Normandy was a culmination of a multi-year development process that exemplifies strategic agility. The US and its Allies made a number of brilliant judgments about the nature of the war on which they were embarking.

First, through a comprehensive assessment of the enemy and the nature of the conflict, US leadership concluded in 1941 that the objective must be the unconditional surrender of the Axis powers. This was an utterly clear and powerfully mobilizing True North, a far-reaching assessment that stood in stark contrast to the judgment of the Soviet leaders, who initially believed peaceful co-existence with the Nazis was not only possible but potentially beneficial. While they were busy working with the Germans on carving Europe into future spheres of influence, the Nazis were preparing for the invasion of the Soviet Union.

The second pivotal decision of the Allied government and military commanders involved the prioritization of joint military efforts and the attendant allocation of resources. The so-called "Europe First" campaign plan stipulated that the majority of Allied resources would be spent to first defeat Nazi Germany while resorting to mostly defensive activities against Japan in the Pacific. The US commitment to this strategy, which was at times akin to Clausewitz's "shield of well-directed blows," held firm despite the trauma of the Japanese attack on Pearl Harbor in December 1941, demonstrating the underlying strength of conviction.

Other critical acts of judgment—including the decision that a cross-channel attack into Europe was the optimal method to defeat Germany—were based on extensive gathering of risk intelligence, a careful evaluation of alternatives, and hard-earned experience with earlier operations.

Having determined its True North and strategy, the US devoted enormous resources and energy to planning, innovating and preparing for the amphibious assault.[173] The pursuit of strategic objectives utilized a rich arsenal of levers. The transformation of the US economy into an "arsenal of democracy" was accompanied by a great deal of engineering innovation, such as the development of specialized amphibious tanks, floating harbors, tide prediction devices, new forms of landing crafts, and flame-throwing and mine-clearing armored vehicles.

The development of versatile vessels and equipment went hand-in-hand with extensive training of the troops, including large-scale war gaming of landings on a number of beaches in England that closely matched the characteristics of the Normandy landing locations. These exercises involved substantial risk, as was tragically demonstrated by Exercise Tiger, conducted with 30,000 American troops as preparation for the landing at Utah beach. A convoy of ships carrying troops was detected and fired on by German fast-attack craft, with the loss of 946 servicemen.[174]

A relentless fight for risk intelligence was also undertaken. In the months preceding the assault, the Allied Expeditionary Air Force conducted thousands of low-altitude reconnaissance flights, collecting detailed images of the terrain, potential obstacles and enemy defenses. Scouting units made innumerous incursions into the heavily patrolled enemy territory in order to gather detailed information about various landing alternatives and surrounding waters. Meanwhile, the Allies' ability to break encoded radio communications in real time provided vital information about the enemy's plans and troop movements.[175]

In parallel, in order to misdirect the Germans about the location and timing of the invasion, the Allies put in place a comprehensive disinformation campaign. Reconnaissance flights were routinely sent along the entire European coastline. Fake radio traffic pinpointed "planned" landing locations across Europe with small army units equipped with dummy tanks, trucks and landing vessels posing as fictitious large armies.[176] Fake networks of informants—many of whom were former German spies turned into double agents—helped reinforce the confusion.[177] Among the tangible accomplishments of the disinformation campaign, the German pullout of significant tank formations in France was one of the most significant, enabling the Allies to secure the initial foothold on the Normandy beaches.

As discussed, government and business levers were used to turn the US into the "arsenal of democracy." The deployment of risk levers—most importantly, the increase in risk appetite—was accompanied by extensive communication about the scale of the effort required for victory, substantially increasing public support for massive financial outlays as well as willingness to incur extensive loss of life. Organizational and communication levers were used to foster cohesion and motivation, gather intelligence and conduct multifaceted disinformation campaigns.

Commander's Intent

On February 12, 1944, the Allied command issued a statement of Commander's Intent to General Eisenhower, appointing him the Supreme Commander of the Allied Expeditionary Forces. Marvelously succinct at a mere eight paragraphs, it is nonetheless comprehensive, serving as a model of clarity combined with latitude. The objectives of the operation, the structure of command, logistics, the division of responsibilities between the forces and the nature of interactions with Allies and the USSR were clearly and comprehensively communicated. The mission was described as follows:

> You will enter the continent of Europe and, in conjunction with the other United Nations, undertake operations aimed at the heart of Germany and the destruction of her armed forces. The date for entering the Continent is the month of May 1944. After adequate channel ports have been secured, exploitation will be directed towards securing an area that will facilitate both ground and air operations against the enemy. Notwithstanding the target date above you will be prepared at any time to take immediate advantage of favorable circumstances, such as withdrawal by the enemy on your front, to effect a reentry into the Continent with such forces as you have available at the time; a general plan for this operation when approved will be furnished for your assistance.

Special Brand of Leadership

In appointing Eisenhower to command, the Allied Chiefs chose with great wisdom. As the *New York Times* later wrote in a tribute to Eisenhower, "He was, in short, a man to be trusted, a man to make the complex simple, to do the job." His leadership qualities comported perfectly with the special brand of leadership we have advocated. The *Times* article goes on to praise his "heart-warming sincerity" and recounts that the way he expressed his beliefs and lived his life "created around him an atmosphere of uncomplicated goodness and uprightness." Radiating goodwill and diplomacy, he preferred persuasion and reconciliation to the blunt exercise of power, which was indispensable in leading the Allied forces to agree to the audacious plan ultimately developed.

Both on battlefields and later in the White House, Eisenhower was said to have a unique ability to "harmonize diverse groups and disparate personalities into a smoothly functioning coalition."[178] He also demonstrated, throughout the war, astute judgment of the leadership talents of his generals. So, it is not surprising he chose "the soldier's General," Omar Bradley, to command the US First Army on D-Day. Quiet, unassuming and capable, Bradley symbolized dependability, common sense and a deep concern for those he led, engendering trust, affection and loyalty. Exceptional as the abilities of both men were, it is important to note that these leadership qualities were deliberately developed in them as they rose through the ranks of command.

The manner in which Eisenhower inspired confidence and impressed upon his commanders and their troops both the gravity and grandeur of their purpose is conveyed potently by his "Order of the Day," speech delivered as both a radio address and a written communique distributed to the troops right before the invasion. We cannot possibly describe the power of his words, so we have included the full order here.

> Soldiers, Sailors, and Airmen of the Allied Expeditionary Force!
>
> You are about to embark upon the Great Crusade, toward which we have striven these many months. The eyes of the

world are upon you. The hope and prayers of liberty-loving people everywhere march with you. In company with our brave Allies and brothers-in-arms on other Fronts, you will bring about the destruction of the German war machine, the elimination of Nazi tyranny over the oppressed peoples of Europe, and security for ourselves in a free world.

Your task will not be an easy one. Your enemy is well trained, well equipped and battle-hardened. He will fight savagely.

But this is the year 1944! Much has happened since the Nazi triumphs of 1940–41. The United Nations have inflicted upon the Germans great defeats, in open battle, man-to-man. Our air offensive has seriously reduced their strength in the air and their capacity to wage war on the ground. Our Home Fronts have given us an overwhelming superiority in weapons and munitions of war, and placed at our disposal great reserves of trained fighting men. The tide has turned! The free men of the world are marching together to Victory!

I have full confidence in your courage, devotion to duty and skill in battle. We will accept nothing less than full Victory!

Good luck! And let us beseech the blessing of Almighty God upon this great and noble undertaking.

There is no substitute for such inspirational, confident and competent leadership. The willingness of a leader to take responsibility for his own actions, and for those under his command, which is critical in fostering a culture of trust, was also admirably displayed by Eisenhower. On the eve of the invasion, he penned a note taking full responsibility in the event of the operation's failure. It states that the decision to attack was based on the best information available, complements the troops on their bravery and devotion to duty, and requests that all blame for the failure be assigned to him *alone*.[179]

Tactical Agility in the Face of Adversity

The fog and friction of battle, and the futility of precise plans, were prominently on display as the invasion got underway. The number of moving pieces was staggering. Thousands of warplanes bombarded the region to clear the way for the landing, while thousands of vessels carried over one hundred fifty thousand troops across the Channel.

Bad weather forced delay from the original date for invasion of June 5. Eisenhower showed great decisiveness by making the excruciating and bold choice to go ahead on June 6, despite the possibility of more stormy weather, rather than waiting for many days until the predictable tidal and moonlight conditions necessary would again prevail. As it turned out, a major storm hit in that later window of days, which would have prevented launch.[180] As feared, strong currents pushed the Allied vessels away from target landing spots. While flotation worked well for the amphibious tanks at some locations, due to high seas at others, out of 290 tanks in total deployed, 42 sank. Improvisation saved many that would likely have met the same fate, which were brought directly to shore.

In spite of the sophisticated disinformation campaign, German commanders viewed Normandy as one of the likely locations and heavily fortified its beaches with mines, anti-tank barriers, barbed-wire obstacles and booby traps. These added substantially to the large casualties on the beaches.[181]

These potentially catastrophic setbacks were overcome through the ingenuity, decisiveness and the will-to-win of the American soldiers who had been so strongly unified around their purpose and equipped with such a clear understanding of goals and measures of success. In the words of our friend Colonel Richard Barnett, a veteran of subsequent wars, "while the concept of agility was seldom discussed or explained within US armed forces, it was fully expected and always practiced by those charged with getting the mission accomplished at all costs."

One of the best illustrations of tactical agility during the invasion, and indeed during the war as a whole, occurred at Pointe du Hoc overlooking Omaha Beach, which was the deadliest point of the amphibious landings. A dominant 100-foot-plus bluff with sheer cliffs plunging into the sea, Pointe du Hoc provided the Germans with excellent observation and fields of fire that would allow them to decimate any force landing on the beach. Allied intelligence had identified powerful artillery pieces emplaced on the bluff, and pre-invasion Allied air attacks pounded the location, but there was no assurance the guns had been taken out.

A formidable mission was assigned to the 2nd and 5th Battalions of the US Army Rangers: to scale the bluffs, seize the position and destroy the guns. The 2nd Battalion would be the first to land and make the initial ascent, and the 5th Battalion would come ashore with the regular infantry of the 29th Infantry Division and fight to link up with 2nd Battalion. Trained under the watchful eyes of British Royal Marine commandos, and already tested in combat, the Rangers diligently studied intelligence, rehearsed and examined every contingency that might prevent them from accomplishing this critical mission. They received newly fielded positional radar devices, amphibious trucks (DUKWs) and other mission-critical equipment. Yet fog and friction would test their agility mightily.

Every Ranger knew exactly what the mission was and understood its purpose and urgency. They trusted each other and the commander, and they willingly accepted the risk. Showing strong leadership, Range Force Commander Colonel Rudder accompanied the force scaling the cliffs.

The plan began to go wrong from the outset. The majority of the ten DUKWs foundered in the heavy seas. The new-fangled radars failed, and the force was driven far off course. In order to make their way to the correct landing spots, the boats had to turn parallel to the coastline, making them wider targets for enemy fire. Many landing craft accompanying the DUKWs were sunk or disabled. Casualties were high before even hitting the beach. Undeterred, the Rangers of the 2nd Battalion who did make it to the beach proceeded to the cliffs under vicious fire from Germans. Once at the cliffs, they found that the scaling ladders were too short to reach the top, and many of the ropes were so sodden and weighted down with sea water that they also could not reach the top when fired from their launchers. The men started their climb, nonetheless, suffering heavy casualties. Those who made it to the top were confronted with yet another challenge: the guns had been moved! With unrelenting commitment to the Commander's Intent, they aggressively patrolled inland until they discovered the camouflaged artillery pieces and destroyed them with thermite grenades.

Meanwhile, mired in the horror of the beach landing, the 5th Ranger Battalion led the decimated regiments of the landing force off the beach and fought to finally conduct a successful link-up with 2nd Battalion on the cliffs above. To this day the Ranger motto is "Rangers Lead the Way," in reference to the gallantry of the 5th Battalion that day. Having secured a foothold on the bluff, the Rangers understood the urgency of holding off any German counteroffensive to regain the ground. They set up roadblocks and beat back numerous bloody German counter-attacks until later relieved by follow-on forces.

The casualties of the two battalions during the mission, including those killed, wounded and captured, were approximately 70 percent. Despite such heavy losses, the troops remained resolute, showing exceptional dedication and will to win, and displaying great dexterity in the face of so much fog and friction, improvising, adapting and overcoming each of the obstacles placed in their way.

Comparable tactical agility was displayed by many other troops during the invasion. Another critical mission was assigned to a force of paratroopers who were dropped into the terrain beyond the beaches in the early morning hours of the invasion. The importance of these airborne missions to the success of the entire operation was so significant that over 13,000 paratroopers were sent, and Eisenhower personally delivered his Order of the Day speech to these troops just before they boarded the planes. A photo of him addressing them became one of the iconic images of Operation Overlord.

The paratroopers encountered substantial challenges right from the start. A combination of factors—including weather, execution mistakes and enemy fire—resulted in a poor accuracy of drops, with troops widely scattered around the large area. What happened next was fascinating. American soldiers—who found themselves in unplanned locations and apart from their team members—spontaneously formed small combat units, assigned leaders based on rank or circumstances, and cohered around actions that were deemed to best advance the overall mission, seizing bridges and strategically important terrain in the process.

Another impressive instance of improvisation was the innovation of "rhino" tanks. Though the Allied forces spent many years assiduously studying the French coastline, after landing, a serious risk-intelligence gap was revealed: the hedgerows that the French countryside was covered with were virtually impassable for the tanks. In response to this unforeseen and potentially disastrous challenge, American soldiers mounted tanks with metal "tusks" made out of whatever materials were on hand.[182] Ironically, the tusks were often from the steel-beam defensive structures the Germans had implanted as defenses on the beaches. Over time, this innovative design became closely studied and productionized on an industrial scale[183] In another example of tactical agility, the carpet bombing of German troops, tanks and positions during Operation Cobra, which took place seven weeks after D-Day, involved the innovative use of B-17 strategic bombers to provide close air support.

In discussing the Battle of Normandy, the military historian Stephen Ambrose has argued that ingenious real-time improvisations by American soldiers should be attributed to the lack of rigid hierarchy in American society.[184] While this may have played a role, in our experience, a lack of hierarchy does not—in and of itself—lead to engagement, coherence and willingness to take risks in ways that lead to viable solutions and innovations. The troops had been well trained and empowered to act with initiative; they were unified around an inspirational True North; and the decisiveness of the leadership and strong culture of trust were vital factors.

The Allied soldiers exhibited all of the hallmarks of agility. They took risks, demonstrated a bias for deliberate action when faced with unexpected challenges and changed tactics as required. They exhibited execution dexterity by deploying a variety of levers. Their actions were purposeful, decisive and grounded in the will to win, leading to effective decentralized execution. The strategic and tactical agility that led to the success of Operation Overlord is still carefully studied and promoted across the US armed forces today.

~

Looking back at different periods in history—with their distinct technologies, economic and political systems, and societal structures—it's striking to realize that the fundamental nature of competitive environments has never really changed. Pervasive uncertainty. The role of chance. The primacy of human factors. The use of force as an extension of politics. Key stakeholders alternating between aggression and risk aversion. All of these factors have been prominently on display for millennia, and they are just as alive and well today.

To confront this reality, armies, governments and businesses have sought, in a determined but often fragmented fashion, to achieve what we describe as agility. Purposeful actions were undertaken to penetrate the uncertainty, shape the competitive playing field, and wrest the initiative from an adversary. As progressively advanced capabilities emerged—from weapons and information technology systems to manufacturing equipment, business methods and financial markets—those who harnessed their power faster and more adroitly gained advantages. Uniforms and flags to distinguish friend from foe; aides on horseback carrying pouches with Commander's Intent in the heat of battle; increasingly robust staffs for planning and assessing operations; and later, yes, corporate brands, mission statements and strategic plans—were all employed to provide the inspiration of a higher purpose and bring order and cohesion to the chaos of the battlefield. And when it all came together, agile teams dominated the disruption of the day, overcame adversity, capitalized on fleeting opportunities...and prevailed.

This time is no different. The fog and friction of the Fourth Industrial Revolution, persistent geopolitical and societal conflict, and an arms race of new technologies are just the modern reincarnations of the challenges that have fueled the humanity's enduring search for agility. As we navigate these powerful forces—and contend with the hedgerows of modernity that upend the most brilliant of plans—any organization and leader can become better positioned to seize the unprecedented possibilities of this new age by investing in agility.

ACKNOWLEDGMENTS

This book would not have been possible without the wisdom, generosity and mentorship of so many colleagues and friends throughout our careers; we wish it were possible to acknowledge all of them here. We owe special gratitude to Wade Barnett, Dr. Pavel Brusilovskiy, George Sparks, Carrie Morgridge and Judith Koval for their thought partnership and innumerable contributions to this project.

We sincerely appreciate the ideas, time and guidance of Amb. John Abizaid, Gen. Martin Dempsey (Ret.), Scott Heiss, Prof. Klaus Schwab, Bill George, Maj. Gen. John Barry (Ret.), Shelly Lazarus, Doug Peterson, Lt. Col. Ryan Shaw (Ret.), Tom Rath, Dr. Mike Davis, Irving Wladawsky-Berger, RuthAnne Dreisbach, Sen. George Mitchell, Prof. Edmund Phelps, Adm. Dennis Blair (Ret.), Gen. Michael Hayden (Ret.), Lord Michael Howard, Col. Richard Barnett (Ret.), Neal Wolin, James Crocker, Mark Ruzycki, David Benson, David Nobel and Dr. William Tracy. We are grateful to Richard Gelfond, Shehu Garba and their colleagues at IMAX and to Hikmet Ersek and his team at Western Union—the case studies on these fascinating companies have enriched the book a great deal. We owe special thanks to Lisa Thomas for her professionalism and extraordinary support in ensuring that this book meets the Department of Defense requirements.

Our sincere appreciation goes to the colleagues who've spent countless hours reviewing the manuscript (and its many painful prior iterations) and offering invaluable critique and advice: Mary McBride, Dr. Rebecca Chopp, Frank Yeary, Ray Thomasson, Merrill Shields, Lakshmi Shyam-Sunder, Amedee Prouvost, Lauren Wright, Daniel Arbess, Nancy Walsh, Elizabeth Concordia, Dr. Philip Joseph, Dr. Donald R. van Deventer, Enrico Dallavecchia, Kevin Hennessey, Jonathan Ewert, Debbie Ball, Stephen McConahey, Gail Klapper, Steve Halstedt, Monty Cleworth and Jamie Stewart.

We were very fortunate to have been surrounded by a publishing dream team. We are deeply grateful to our Missionday publisher Dr. Piotr Juszkiewicz for believing in this project and for tirelessly working with us throughout the process; to our editor Emily Loose for her brilliant editing and guidance—and for challenging us to leave no stone unturned (or unexplained); to Barbara Henricks, Pamela Peterson and Kenneth Gillett for shaping and masterfully executing the marketing and strategic communications strategy; to AuthorScope, and especially Gary Lindberg and Beth Williams, for their diligence and professionalism in book design, copyediting, indexing and production; and to Barbara Mack, Kyle Kremiller and Sohini Bandopadhyay for fastidious editorial and research assistance.

Last but certainly not least, we thank our families for their love and infinite support and patience throughout this long, don't-try-it-at-home en-deavor. We dedicate this book to them.

ENDNOTES

Chapter 1: The Agility Mission

1   Scott Anthony, S. Patrick Viguerie and Andrew Waldeck, "Corporate Longevity: Turbulence Ahead for Large Organizations," Innosight Executive Briefing (Spring 2016), http://bit.ly/2VVg-Gty.

2   Parts of this section are based on Charles Jacoby, Jr., with Ryan Shaw, "Strategic Agility: Theory and Practice," *Joint Force Quarterly*, 81 (2016), http://bit.ly/2QwhxzL. Included by permission.

3   As we'll elaborate in Chapter 9, some of this language builds on that in Stephen Covey's *The Speed of Trust* (Free Press; Reprint edition October 17, 2006) and *Smart Trust (*Free Press; Reprint edition January 10, 2012).

4   The first was the drawdown of US military power after the Vietnam War. After the success of the first Gulf War of 1990–91 and the fall of the Berlin Wall later in 1991, another major drawdown of forces was ordered. Most recent drawdown was the result of the 2011 Budget Control Act that reduced force structure and readiness while the major conflicts in Iraq and Afghanistan were still going on.

Chapter 2: Fog, Friction and the Edge of Chaos

5   Leo Tolstoy, *War and Peace* (Project Gutenberg, Book 10, Chapter XXXIII, accessed at http://bit.ly/2XaGnHX). Context from: Keith Green, "Complex Adaptive Systems in Military Analysis," Institute for Defense Analyses, May 2011.

6   Throughout our book, Clausewitz quotes are from Carl von Clausewitz, *On War*, ed. and trans. Michael Howard and Peter Paret (Princeton, NJ: Princeton University Press, 1976, 1984).

7   Klaus Schwab, "The Fourth Industrial Revolution: What It Means and How to Respond," *Foreign Affairs*, December 12, 2015.

8   *Operations*: Field Manual 3-0, US Department of the Army.

9   Hybrid warfare combines conventional military capabilities with information warfare, cyber warfare, proxy warfare and sponsorship of terrorism.

10   We are grateful to Dr. William Tracy of the Santa Fe Institute for his insights on the properties of complex adaptive systems.

11   This has become increasingly self-evident as globalization and interconnectedness of political, economic, financial and business environments around the world have turned our operating environment into one giant complex adaptive system.

12   Green, "Complex Adaptive Systems in Military Analysis," p. 1-1.

13   James Mackintosh, "$2 Trillion Later, Does the Fed Even Know if Quantitative Easing Worked?" *Wall Street Journal*, September 21, 2017. Quantitative easing programs involve purchases of long-maturity fixed income instruments and aim to keep interest rates low and yield curves flat. These programs belong to a category of actions where policy makers attempt to shield societies from adversity and volatility, often causing even greater problems and instability in the long-term.

14   Niall Ferguson, "Complexity and Collapse," *Foreign Affairs* (March/April 2010), https://fam.ag/2JNK4Am.

15   A gradual increase in computing power that eventually leads to dramatic societal changes is another example of an endogenous process. Exogenous shocks can sometimes catalyze endogenous processes as well.

16   David M. Keithly and Stephen P. Ferris, "*Auftragstaktik*, or Directive Control, in Joint and Combined Operations," *Parameters/U.S. Army War College Quarterly* (Autumn 1999), pp. 118–33.

17   Daniel Kahneman, *Thinking, Fast and Slow* (Farrar, Straus and Giroux, 2011), pp. 263, 284–285, 303, 342, 348–349.

18   Daniel Kahneman and Amos Tversky, "Prospect Theory: An Analysis of Decision under Risk," Econometrica 47, no. 2 (March 1979): pp. 263–292.

19   IMAX currently trades on the New York Stock Exchange and the Hong Kong Stock Exchange.

20   See http://bit.ly/2Quzizx.

21   In *Blue Ocean Strategy*, W. C. Kim and R. Mauborgne define red oceans as overcrowded marketplaces where players are engaged in a hand-to-hand combat over commoditized products and a limited profit pool. In contrast, blue oceans are the new and uncontested marketplaces. W. C. Kim and R. Mauborgne, *Blue Ocean Strategy* (Harvard Business Review Press; Expanded edition January 20, 2014).

22   For example, agility was one of the tenets of AirLand Battle Doctrine that approached a definition but was focused at the tactical and operational level and did not usefully distinguish agility from speed (see *Department of the Army Historical Summary: FY1989*, p. 46).

23   Green, "Complex Adaptive Systems in Military Analysis," p. 1–6.

Chapter 3: The Essence of Agility

24   Hal Gregersen, "Busting the CEO Bubble," Harvard Business Review (March/April 2017), https://hbr.org/2017/03/bursting-the-ceo-bubble.

25   Mark Gilbert, "Devouring Capitalism," Bloomberg.com, August 4, 2017.

26   Throughout the book, in the case studies that happened before we started working together, "we" refers to Leo and his team at Tilman & Company.

27   http://www.businessdictionary.com/definition/adaptability.html.

28   https://www.merriam-webster.com/dictionary/resilience.

29 https://www.dictionary.com/browse/flexible.

30 https://en.oxforddictionaries.com/definition/dynamism.

31 Compare The Principles of War of different militaries (http://bit.ly/2wyFTiZ) vis-à-vis the use of "agility" in the *Joint Force 2020* vision cited in Chapter 7.

32 McKinsey & Company Publication, "The keys to organizational agility," 2015, https://mck.co/2I5aASo.

Chapter 4: Risk Intelligence

33 Wilson Liu and Martin Pergler, "Concrete steps for CFOs to improve strategic risk management," McKinsey Working Papers on Risk, no. 44 (2013).

34 Leo Tilman, "Risk Intelligence: A Bedrock of Dynamism and Lasting Value Creation," *European Financial Review* (2013).

35 Some of the most effective uses of business intelligence involve a careful integration of data analyses with subjective expert judgment. See, for example, Pavel Brusilovskiy and Leo Tilman, "Incorporating expert judgment into multivariate polynomial modeling," *Decision Support Systems* (1996).

36 Leo also aimed to address the intellectual and operational limitations of prior definitions of risk intelligence. For example, David Apgar's book *Risk Intelligence* described risk intelligence as the capacity to learn about risk from experience, which lacked operational clarity and blinded decision makers to paradigm shifts and black swans. Dylan Evans' understanding of risk intelligence as the ability to accurately estimate probabilities suffered from all the pitfalls of predicting the unknowable future we discussed in Chapter 3. See Dylan Evans, *Risk Intelligence: How to Live with Uncertainty* (New York: Free Press, 2012), p. 288.

37 Some organizations consider adversaries a driver of strategic risk and take explicit actions to neutralize competitors and exploit their mistakes. As a rule, however, strategic risk is managed outside of formal risk management processes and in isolation from other risks.

38 For example, no commercially viable Comanche helicopters were delivered after twenty-two years and $7 billion in expenditures. See Dan Ward, "Real Lessons from an Unreal Helicopter," time.com, May 25, 2012, http://bit.ly/2HLaYGR.

39 Stephen Shankland, "IBM grabs consulting giant for $3.5 billion," cnet.com, July 31, 2002, https://cnet.co/2Qwj6h7.

40 Our approach is consistent with and complementary to the accepted definition of risk described in the International Standard ISO 31000 "Risk management—Principles and Guidelines" (2009).

41 Jessica Silver-Greenberg and Peter Eavis, "JPMorgan Discloses $2 Billion in Trading Losses," nytimes.com, May 10, 2012.

42 Risk is the possibility of negative outcomes, or the left side of probability distribution. From this perspective, a stock market investment is a vulnerability because it may lose value. However, the same stock market investment can also be described as an asset that can be used to generate gains, the right side of the probability distribution. In other words, thanks to the role of chance, the same set of exposures, that we can call either vulnerabilities or assets, can generate both positive and negative consequences.

43 In practice, when confronting uncertainty, organizations often use the subjective judgment of experts to assign likelihoods to future events that don't have repeatable historical precedents. We have discussed the dangers of these practices in the earlier chapters.

44 By using different data and assumptions, we can understand how probability distributions linked to our risk equations can change across different environments, affecting both likelihoods and consequences of risk.

45 Stephen Stapczynski and Chisaki Watanabe, "Japan Court Allows Nuclear Reactor to Reopen in Boost to Abe's Energy Push," bloomberg.com, September 25, 2018, https://bloom.bg/2JKzZ7d.

46 Source: Investigation Committee on the Accident at the Fukushima Nuclear Power Stations of Tokyo Electric Power Company, http://bit.ly/2WjpCcc.

Chapter 5: What Business Are We In?

47 In addition to his lack of understanding of the business Bear Stearns was actually in, Cayne, who personally lost over a billion dollars when the firm collapsed, also exemplified a fascinating phenomenon described by Daniel Kahneman. Cayne was one of those executives who owned a disproportionate amount of stock in their own companies—all while steering the firm to ruin. This indicates that such executives often take excessive risks not because they are playing with other people's money, but because of their unwarranted overconfidence (Kahneman, *Thinking, Fast and Slow*, p. 258).

48 In a fire sale, Bear Stearns and Merrill Lynch were merged into larger rivals. Lehman Brothers' bankruptcy put the entire global economic and financial system on the verge of collapse. Goldman Sachs, whose balance sheet was stronger to begin with, survived due to effective crisis management and some assistance from investors and regulators (Chapter 10). It seemed that Morgan Stanley just got lucky, as letting Goldman Sachs become a sole surviving investment bank would have been too conspicuous.

49 Which Leo referred to in *Financial Darwinism* as risk-based business models, thus establishing a direct connection between risk and the dominant aspects of performance, such as growth, profitability and equity valuation.

50 For confidentiality reasons, some of the details in this example have been modified.

51 Such practices may be warranted when the risks in question are truly independent from each other and can be managed via diversification. For large and complex organizations, this, in our experience, is rare.

52 Timeframe: 2012–16. Source: http://bit.ly/2I3iFqM.

53 NFL Concussions Fast Facts, cnn.com, August 26, 2018, https://cnn.it/2JMedA5. Mark Freeman, "New Helmet Rule Could Make NFL Unrecognizable," bleacherreport.com, http://bit.ly/2HI7i8F.

54 The concept of a static business model was originally inspired by our experience of advising asset managers. Consider, for example, a pension fund or a college endowment whose investment portfolio is comprised of stocks and bonds. If the economy is expected to go into a recession, the fund's investment committee may decide to sell stocks of luxury goods or car manufacturers and use the proceeds to buy defensive stocks, such as utilities or consumer staples. Using a similar rationale, portfolios of high-yield corporate bonds may be substituted with US Treasuries. When the economy is expected to recover, the trade may be reversed. Notice that while the individual holdings are changed, *directional* exposures to equity and fixed income markets remain the same. Thus, despite the seemingly thoughtful rebalancing, the fund's performance will suffer in a recession when entire stock markets lose value. Considering

that assets and liabilities of pension funds are often mismatched (durations of pension funds' investment portfolios are usually much shorter than those of their liabilities), the decline in interest rates is likely to result in additional losses.

55 Alan Greenspan, "Never Saw It Coming," *Foreign Affairs*, November 2013.

56 These attempts to sell assets cause further price declines.

57 Sources of information are as follows. Revenues and their decomposition: company disclosures. Percentage of global digital ad revenues and mechanics of advertising business model: Rani Molla, "Google leads the world in digital and mobile ad revenue," vox.com, July 24, 2017, http://bit.ly/2KbuUEs. Revenue equation: Ben Parr, "The Google Revenue Equation, and Why Google's Building Chrome OS," mashable.com, July 11, 2009, http://bit.ly/2KeVUCL. Company description: Wikipedia.

58 Suzanne Vranica, "Amazon's Rise in Ad Searches Dents Google's Dominance," *Wall Street Journal*, April 4, 2019, https://on.wsj.com/2EE0A1p.

59 John McKinnon and Jeff Horwitz, "HUD Action Against Facebook Signals Trouble for Other Platforms," *Wall Street Journal*, March 28, 2019, https://on.wsj.com/312oKwq.

60 Numbers quoted in this paragraph are from Austan Goolsbee and Alan Krueger, "A Retrospective Look at Rescuing and Restructuring General Motors and Chrysler," *Journal of Economic Perspectives* 29, no. 2 (Spring 2015): pp. 3–24, http://bit.ly/2Wrbd1Z.

61 See Steven Metz, "Learning from Iraq: Counterinsurgency in American Strategy," SSI/US Army War College, January 2007, http://bit.ly/2EFJpNe.

62 Tom Shean, "How Wachovia came crashing down," pilotonline.com, Oct. 5, 2008, http://bit.ly/2Wv6sEl. "Rick Rothacker, $5 billion withdrawn in one day in silent run," *The Charlotte Observer*, Oct. 11, 2008.

63 Ashley Parker, "Romney Campaigns at Failed Solyndra Factory," nytimes.com, May 31, 2012, https://nyti.ms/30OyUAF.

64 After Solyndra delivered over $100 million in revenues in both 2009 and 2010, things suddenly changed. The price of one of the main ingredients for technologies used by Solyndra's competitors dropped by nearly 90 percent. With the new manufacturing cost structure in place, Solyndra's technology became instantly non-economical.

65 http://bit.ly/2MfXRSg.

66 Leo Tilman and Al Puchala, "Risk Intelligence: A Framework for Active Credit Portfolio Management and Policy Effectiveness," Presentation to the Federal Credit Policy Council, US Treasury, February 7, 2014.

67 We are grateful to Mary Miller, the Undersecretary of US Treasury at the time, for her thought partnership throughout this process.

68 Robert Kegan, *In Over Our Heads: The Mental Demands of Modern Life* (Cambridge: Harvard University Press, 1994), as well as J. G. Berger, B. Hasegawa, J. Hammerman and R. Kegan, "How consciousness develops adequate complexity to deal with a complex world: The subject-object theory of Robert Kegan," (2007). Retrieved from http://bit.ly/2QANqY6. We are grateful to our colleague David Noble for his insights on this topic.

Chapter 6: The Risk Levers of Agility

69 https://bbc.in/2I7M1o0.

70 http://bit.ly/2WDf500.

71 http://bit.ly/2HLdyg1.

72 http://bit.ly/2QwY7e0 and http://bit.ly/2Mh5ojy.

73 As part of their deep personal involvement, the battlefield circulation by senior military commanders is essential because it enables them to gain a perspective that may be very different from what they receive from the subordinates. This process can be greatly enhanced by what is known in the military as a *directed telescope*: a team of dedicated, highly qualified associates that serve, in the words of military analyst Gary Griffin, as an "extension" of the leader's mind in the process of penetrating fog and friction http://bit.ly/2I7dXZb.

74 Interestingly, as with the observer principle in physics where the act of observation may affect the phenomenon we are studying, our fight for risk intelligence can and often does affect our operating environment in unexpected ways, exacerbating fog and friction, http://bit.ly/2I7dXZb.

75 This increasingly includes elaborate uses of the propaganda masked as scientific method, http://bit.ly/2XcVl0d.

76 Quantifiable risks are presented in terms of economic capital: the fifth percentile of the annual probability distribution for both individual and aggregate risks.

77 Colors are related to risk limits and governance protocols discussed shortly.

78 The dispersion (*volatility*) of potential outcomes is implicit in the concept of risk. Risks with large underlying volatilities can manifest themselves in severe losses or extraordinary gains, whereas less volatile risks will likely lead to more limited positive and negative consequences. As mentioned before, the dispersion of positive and negative outcomes is not necessarily symmetric: some risks may have much more upside than the downside, and vice versa. Aggregate risk assessments depend on the assumptions about volatilities and correlations of individual risks. This facet of risk intelligence is especially complex because changes in the environment can significantly alter the relationships between different risks as well as their volatilities. For example, systematic financial risks tend to become more volatile and correlated during economic shocks and financial crises. Meanwhile, long periods of tranquility often witness less synchronized and less volatile movements of different risk factors.

79 This can be done by presenting baseline estimates of risk alongside carefully crafted historical and hypothetical scenarios across different horizons. This will reflect the fact that all components of risk—vulnerabilities, likelihoods, consequences, volatilities and correlations—change with environments and evolve over time. The assessment of the data quality can be included as well. When a financial risk is measured on a granular level, an organization's exposure is usually mapped onto the probability distribution of an observable market factor, such as an interest rate, a stock market index or implied volatility of an option. In addition to the overall estimate of risk depicted on the risk radar, these market drivers of risk can serve as effective early warning indicators.

80 For example, yellow to mid-level executives, orange to C-suite executives, and red to the board of directors.

81 Equities can be further subdivided by country, industry and capitalization; interest rates can be stratified by country and maturity; and credit risks can be stratified by country, sector and maturity. Empowering stakeholders with this type of risk information was discussed in Tilman, "Corporate Risk Scorecard," *Barrons*, http://bit.ly/2wGlXde.

82 We are grateful to Dr. Pavel Brusilovskiy for his ideas on classifying different types of uncertainty.

83   In some circumstances, this process can be empowered by marrying subjective expert judgment and data analysis. We are grateful to Owen Tilman for his insights on 1) the creative role of risk intelligence and risk managers in scenario generation, and 2) the role of environmental knowledge and preparedness—in his words, "the environment as friend or foe"—in fostering agility.

84   http://bit.ly/2YVf4Sn; https://cnn.it/2W3whaF.

85   Advances in gene editing can be used to create man-made pandemics directed at people or agriculture, which can be incorporated into the risk radar.

86   The American Enterprise Institute's Critical Threats Project serves as a good example of specific domain expertise.

87   In this regard, traditional concepts of optimality can be used: achieving the best possible outcome for a given level of risk or achieving a particular outcome with the smallest possible amount of risk.

88   Making risk appetite and risk budgeting a cornerstone of decision-making and resource allocation across organizational levels is both powerful and challenging. By its very nature, the total amount of risk is a combination of quantitative and qualitative factors—and a mix of risk and uncertainty. Advances in risk management and rapidly increasing computing power are making it increasingly possible to aggregate a vast array of individual exposures across financial, operational, cybersecurity, and other risks into meaningful summary measures, such as economic capital.

89   "FEMA Seeks to Shift Risk," *Wall Street Journal*, April 5, 2018.

90   http://bit.ly/2WeqdAX.

Chapter 7: Command, Control and Radical Empowerment

91   Stephen Bungay, "The road to mission command: The genesis of a command philosophy," *The British Army Review*, 2005, p. 137, as quoted by Keith Stewart, "The Evolution of Command Approach," http://bit.ly/2Z1P2gt.

92   Trevor Dupuy, *The Evolution of Weapons and Warfare* (Indianapolis: Bobbs-Merrill, 1980), as quoted by Keith Stewart, "The Evolution of Command Approach," p. 4.

93   Keith Stewart, "The Evolution of Command Approach," p. 5.

94   http://bit.ly/2VYFi4D.

95   Originally from Joint Publication 3-0, *Joint Operations* as referenced in https://mwi.usma.edu/1883-2/.

96   It is where conditions are set to begin subsequent "sequels" to the operation or follow-on missions. Anticipating "what's next" is an essential role of the commander.

97   http://bit.ly/2XdxHkf.

98   In another example, in 2007 Chuck took command of I Corps (the "America's Corps"), rebuilt it into a premier fighting organization, and then in 2009 took it as warfighting headquarters to Iraq. Given the sheer size, scope and the progression of different missions spanning several years—sustaining the post-counterinsurgency drop in violence, paving the way to democratic elections, creating a trusted partnership between American and Iraqi forces and facilitating a successful American withdrawal—shaping Commander's Intent at the highest operational level and fostering a clear understanding and buy-in of the objectives and key tasks across the multinational force of over 135,000 service members was critical.

99   As emphasized in Leo Tilman, Stephen Kosslyn and G. Wayne Miller, "Brain as a Business Model," *European Financial Review* (2014), "Contrary to the cultural myth, there is no scientific evidence that the left hemisphere of the human brain is analytical and logical while the right one is intuitive and creative. These two brain systems are not independent agents free to operate in isolation. Nobody is truly left-brained or right-brained." Parts of this article are quoted throughout this section and included by permission." http://bit.ly/2KuVKHN

100   See https://amzn.to/2JKT4Go and Tilman, Kosslyn and Miller, "Brain as a Business Model." The original frameworks were developed by Kosslyn, and Tilman and Kosslyn, respectively; and G. Wayne Miller was a co-author of both publications.

101   http://bit.ly/2Xm4Eep

102   The cognitive mode perspective can be also quite helpful in structuring effective and complementary teams, since all team members have a dominant cognitive mode. For example, risk managers, intelligence officers and accountants are often described as fact-based, inductive, pessimistic, "world as it is" perceivers. When leaders operating in mover or stimulator modes, as is often the case, are informed, and cautioned, by empowered teams of perceivers, the collaborative whole is often much greater than the sum of its parts.

103   Similarly, advertising agencies and movie studios often emphasize a decentralized, bottom-up creative process that some of them describe as "harnessing the slices of genius."

Chapter 8: Operationalized Strategic Vision

104   Think of Facebook's activities in the wake of the revelations about fake accounts and violations of users' privacy in 2018.

105   Throughout this chapter, quotes regarding Amazon in this section are from the company's 1997 letter to shareholders and other public disclosures.

106   McKinsey https://mck.co/2MdwuYR referring to John Graham, Campbell Harvey and Shiva Rajgopal, "Value destruction and financial reporting decisions," *Financial Analysts Journal* 62, no. 6 (2006): 27–39.

107   When this is done with respect to reputational or legal risks, this is simply an expression of the organization's values and ethical standards. However, when this applies to financial or business risks, such defensive posture also eliminates the upside of risk. Simply put, it deprives decision makers of the risk levers that may become essential in the future.

108   This principle helps prevent destructive behaviors where companies start "competing on price" or, in the language of finance, participating in "crowded trades" where one is not adequately compensated for an inherent risk and suffers huge losses when everyone rushes to the door at the same time.

109   Alan C. Greenberg, *Memos from the Chairman* (Workman Publishing Company, 1996), p. 97.

110   Paul Zak, *Trust Factor: The Science of Creating High-Performance Companies* (AMACOM, 2017), p. 76.

111   Ace Greenberg, *Memos from the Chairman*, excerpts from across the book.

112   For example, an organization may be directed to invest in industrial-strength integrated processes—because the inefficiency and operational risks of a patchwork of disparate systems glued together by human intervention are deemed unacceptable.

113   http://bit.ly/2K9FUlw.

114 To reflect the nature of its risk-taking, the company's investment process and organizational structures were subsequently made more centralized, with aggregate risk metrics playing a greater role in asset allocation decisions.

115 This discussion is also relevant to situations where leaders own the risk and outcomes but are unable to set the appropriate boundaries of initiative. For example, as discussed in Chapter 5, US government agencies are among the biggest risk-takers in the world who routinely make billions of dollars' worth of loans and investments to advance public policy. Their boundaries of initiative are broadly defined by appropriation budgets and scopes of activities, but they have significant discretion in determining the amount of risk. The US Treasury is the ultimate steward of public assets and the owner of that risk, but it has no control over the activities of other agencies and cannot impose risk limits it might deem appropriate. The recent efforts by US Treasury to understand the country's overall portfolio of risks were important steps toward fostering risk intelligence and agility in such a setting. Asset owners who employ a variety of independent investment managers often find themselves in similar situations. In such cases, the so-called "overlay" strategies that rebalance the portfolio of risks on the organization-wide level may be required, as described in Bennett Golub and Leo Tilman, *Risk Management: Approaches for Fixed Income Markets* (Wiley: 2000), https://amzn.to/31fv3gj. This approach is usually applied to the management of financial risks.

116 Such as fire attack, search and rescue, or water supply.

117 This presents a sharp contrast to typical corporate practices that are much less dynamic. Corporate orgcharts are designed to reflect the company's business model and accepted best practices at a moment in time. Eventually, they become ingrained in processes, strategic plans, metrics, and cultures. Unless companies are willing to significantly readjust organizational structures when environments change, which can be very disruptive, their agility will be impaired.

118 http://bit.ly/2JLpel0.

Chapter 9: Decisiveness

119 H. R. McMaster, *Dereliction of Duty: Johnson, McNamara, the Joint Chiefs of Staff, and the Lies That Led to Vietnam* (Harper, 1997).

120 Harry Summers, *American Strategy in Vietnam: A Critical Analysis* (Dover Publications: 2012) and *On Strategy: The Vietnam War in Context* (Presidio Press: reissue edition 2009).

121 In a well-known example, strategic asset allocation is the single most powerful determinant of the overall performance of traditional asset managers.

122 John Rhodehamel, *George Washington: The Wonder of the Age* (Yale University Press: 2017).

123 The expression "our leaders lost their way" has come up numerous times. Interestingly, the judge in the so-called Bridgegate scandal used a similar language in his sentencing comments, saying that the defendants "got caught up in a culture and an environment that lost its way." https://nyp.st/2VZvDuB.

124 A related recent public example involves the alleged misdeeds by the ride-hailing pioneer Uber Technologies, including industrial espionage, bribery, obstruction of justice, as well as workplace and sexual harassment. While the company's policies and controls have likely contributed to the problems, the absence of True North appears to have been important. Uber's original core values focused on customer "obsession," long-term thinking, bold risk-taking, innovation,

inspiration, perseverance and hard work. The imperatives of character and morality were entirely absent. Only at the end of 2017 did the company's core values were amended to say: "We do the right thing. Period." https://on.wsj.com/2W2Glei, https://on.wsj.com/2Mdy7FX.

125 Jonathan Haidt, *The Righteous Mind* (Vintage: 2012), pp. 205–206, 209–210, 219–220.

126 http://bit.ly/2I9OQER.

127 http://bit.ly/2XdPF5V.

128 Ray Dalio: http://bit.ly/2Z0rUir; Jeffreyf Sonnenfeld: http://bit.ly/2WgskUX; Amazon.com: http://bit.ly/2YRVYMQ; Salesforce: http://bit.ly/2WgsrQn.

129 David Hackett Fischer, "Washington's Crossing" and C. DeMuth "The Method in Trump's Tumult," *Wall Street Journal*, February 11–12, 2017.

130 Kahneman, *Thinking, Fast and Slow*, pp. 212, 160. Kahneman's concept of the "planning fallacy" is a great case in point: by adding additional details to strategic or contingency plans, scenarios are simultaneously made more coherent and plausible—and less probable.

131 https://amzn.to/30OFze9.

132 Of course, as opposed to honest mistakes, violations of the norms must be consistently and swiftly punished. This includes attempts to humiliate or demean colleagues under the disguise of honesty and transparency—a sure way to decimate the Forum of Truth, engagement and trust.

133 We owe this observation to Maj. General John Barry who we introduced in the previous chapters.

134 A number of multidisciplinary approaches have proven useful in this regard, like the "red team/ blue team" approach to war games originally conceived by the national security community (http://bit.ly/2HJwMm4), as well as the so-called *premortems*— formal analyses that imagine that an initiative has failed and then perform a typical postmortem (http://bit.ly/2KdBdHx).

135 Charles Darwin, *The descent of man, and selection related to sex* (London: John Murray). As a noteworthy case in point, the executive team of a leading US company that we worked with was shocked to discover that the firm's lack of innovation stemmed not from employees' anxiety about undermining their bonuses or promotions if ideas didn't work, but rather a fear of "losing face" in front of their superiors and colleagues, http://bit.ly/2I5nAra.

136 Kahneman, *Thinking, Fast and Slow*, pp. 413 and 225.

137 Verizon presentation at the Goldman Sachs investor conference (2017).

138 http://bit.ly/2Wefarg. Interestingly, Shiller has also argued that the new "post-truth" culture dominated by modern information technology and social media may be even more susceptible to non-factual narratives. Narrative psychology is also related to the psychologists' concept of framing, as exemplified by the work of Thaler, Kahneman and Tversky.

139 http://bit.ly/2WwUIXB.

140 Darwin, *The descent of man*, p. 88.

141 Zak, *Trust Factor: The Science of Creating High-Performance Companies*, discussed throughout the book.

142 Zak, *Trust Factor: The Science of Creating High-Performance Companies*, pp. 45, 50, who also notes that regular feedback on performance builds neural pathways in the brain that help adapt behaviors to meet goals. In other psychological research, expectations of excellence have shown to improve performance, while a visible lack of confidence in people's abilities yielded

inferior results. The *realism* of expectations proved important as well, since attempts to reach unreasonable targets tend to lead to unethical choices, especially when employees feel pressured to achieve results at all costs.

143 Kahneman, *Thinking, Fast and Slow*, pp. 46, 217, 418.

144 Haidt, *The Righteous Mind*, pp. 74–76, 90–91.

145 Haidt, *The Righteous Mind*, pp. 102, 144, 238.

146 https://on.wsj.com/2Kc63Ab.

147 The relative importance of these moral foundations depends on the nature of the organization's business and the prevailing culture (for instance, societal emphasis on individualism vs. community). Thus, members of the armed forces, law enforcement and fire service willingly give up certain rights to join the organization where loyalty, dependability and cohesion are more important than individual liberty.

148 Some of the preventive strategies come in the form of the enhancement and enforcement of fire codes.

149 This is not meant to imply that fire service leaders are not rigorously qualified and selected. Our comments are focused on the dynamic where rank-and-file gravitate to the leaders they respect and trust, exemplifying the concept of "leadership as followership."

150 A case in point is a change in the method adopted for combatting fire in a burning building. Research showed that if the water is directed at the ceiling at the right angle and with the right nozzle pattern, it can effectively diminish fire while also improving the safety of the firefighters. The prior approach was to send firefighters immediately into the building to assess the situation. Resistance to the change was due in part to the long-held pride that real firefighters have the courage to put their life on the line. The objection was also made that the old method had been so successful for so many years. Due to the culture of respect within the service, the well-demonstrated authority of the leadership, and the evidence-based and culturally-sensitive discussion of the need to change, buy-in was achieved.

151 Stephen M. R. Covey, *The Speed of Trust*.

Chapter 10: Execution Dexterity

152 Unless stated otherwise, all quotes in this section are from FDR's original speech.

153 This quote and some of Marshall's rationale are based on http://bit.ly/2I83oF4.

154 http://bit.ly/2VUX5tq.

155 Ibid.

156 http://bit.ly/2Keez1U.

157 Ibid Prospect.org, http://bit.ly/2VUX5tq.

158 https://cnn.it/2wCrxOZ.

159 These insurance strategies required significant investment and were implemented via credit default swaps.

160 http://bit.ly/2Mguu2f.

161 http://bit.ly/2XdPJTm.

162 https://on.wsj.com/2WjDXdS.

163 https://on.wsj.com/2wtJj6G.

164 Yaakov Katz and Amir Bohbot, *The Weapon Wizards* (St. Martin's Press, 2017), p. 8, https://amzn.to/2I83E70.

165 "Montenegro: Russia involved in attempted coup," By Milena Veselinovic and Darran Simon, CNN, February 21, 2017. https://cnn.it/2XilCKs; https://cnn.it/2VYVDWU; https://on.wsj.com/2Weg1lu; https://on.wsj.com/30V3cl6; http://bit.ly/2W1SmpY; https://on.wsj.com/30LUBkG; https://on.wsj.com/2HKUA9I. See Rumer and Weiss, "Putin's Russia is Going Global", *Wall Street Journal*, August 5–6, 2017.

166 See also: https://cnnmon.ie/2WwWzWX.

167 Nathan Hodge and Julian Barnes, "The New Cold War Pits a US General Against His Longtime Russian Nemesis," *Wall Street Journal*, June 16, 2017. https://on.wsj.com/2I5qfBa.

168 Ibid.

Chapter 11: Planning for Agility

169 At the time, a single telegram could cost up to $20.

170 Corporate partnerships for the kiosks included Walgreens in the United States, WH Smith in the United Kingdom, and FranPrix in France.

171 Compliance funding increased by more than 200 percent between 2011 and 2016.

172 Total downloads as of year-end 2016. Over 60 percent of WU.com transactions are now initiated on a mobile device.

173 US Department of the Navy, Naval History and Heritage Command. "D-Day, the Normandy Invasion," June 6–25, 1944.

174 http://bit.ly/2wurx3n.

175 Andrew Whitmarsh, *D-Day in Photographs* (Stroud: The History Press, 2009).

176 Anthony Cave Brown, *Bodyguard of Lies: The Extraordinary True Story Behind D-Day.* (Guilford, CT: Globe Pequot, 2007, 1975).

177 Antony Beevor, *D-Day: The Battle for Normandy* (New York; Toronto: Viking, 2009).

178 https://nyti.ms/2KefmzU.

179 Sources: Order of the Day, National Archives; "in case of failure:" http://bit.ly/2JO20Ld; NYT: https://nyti.ms/2VWJvpy.

180 http://bit.ly/2wqVCAD.

181 Martin Gilbert, *The Second World War: A Complete History* (New York: H. Holt, 1989). https://amzn.to/2WetrEC.

182 Steven Zaloga, *Armored Champion: The Top Tanks of World War II* (Mechanicsburg, PA: Stackpole Books, 2015), https://amzn.to/2MiJjkN.

183 We would like to thank Dr. Mike Davis for attracting our attention to this example of agility and providing invaluable insights.

184 Stephen Ambrose, *D-Day: June 6, 1944, The Climactic Battle of World War II* (New York: Simon & Schuster, reprint edition 1995).

INDEX